The American University
Alma Mater & Fight Song

THE AMERICAN UNIVERSITY
ALMA MATER & FIGHT SONG

Abdul Karim Bangura

Writers Club Press
San Jose New York Lincoln Shanghai

The American University Alma Mater & Fight Song

Writers Club Press
an imprint of iUniverse, Inc.

For information address:
iUniverse, Inc.
5220 S. 16th St., Suite 200
Lincoln, NE 68512
www.iuniverse.com

ISBN: 0-595-22488-1

Printed in the United States of America

The only thing that one can do in opening a university is to say we wish to add one more means of emancipating the human mind—emancipating it from fear, from misunderstanding—emancipating it from the dark and leading it into the light.

Woodrow Wilson
American University's Official Opening Ceremony, May 27, 1914

Go Eagles!

Contents

Acknowledgments

I, and hopefully many readers, owe gratitude to:

American University students for listening to and providing useful comments on the subject. Asking difficult questions often leads to better answers.

Kate Lundgren Murtaugh and Shanelle Wells, for tirelessly assisting with the research and smoothing out technical rough spots.

George Arnold (American University Archivist) and Ignacio Moreno (Assistant American University Archivist), for unselfishly providing archival research support.

Diana Marie Kelly, Fatmata Aminata Bangura, Isatu Ramatu Bangura, and the numerous other members of the various families to which I belong, for offering encouragement and prayers.

Notation Conventions

A, B, C Sentential variables

p, q, r   Sentential variables

$A(e_1)$ Ad hoc notation for a sentential variable that Indicates the occurrence of an expression e_1 in a sentence A

F, G   Predicate constants, as in $F(X)$

a, b, c   Individual constants; also persons in expressions like 'a knows that p'

x, y, z   Individual variables

v   Inclusive disjunction

V   Exclusive disjunction

~   Negation

→   Material conditional

=   Identity

∈   Is an element of a set

{ }   Sets

⊩   Entailment

>>	Presupposes
+>	Implicates
K	Speaker knows that; thus Kp = speaker Knows that p
P	Epistemic possibility for speaker; thus Pp = p is compatible with all that the speaker knows

The American University Alma Mater & Fight Song

Alma Mater

Our college years soon behind us, into shadows of the past.
So will the years often find us: recalling days that flew so fast.
Come, come, days that we treasure, we live in you!
We yearn now for all the pleasures of college we knew!
Friendships will always bind us and remind us of Red, White
and Blue!
Come, days, fullest in measures of our AU!

By: John M. Houston and Clair S. Atland, 1931
Revised and Arranged by: David Horne, 1999

Fight Song

All hail the might AU Eagles!
When there's a fight we'll see it through!
You can be sure we'll be triumphant, when we hear red, white
and blue.
All hail the might AU Eagles!
We'll conquer ev'ry enemy!
So lets all join in and give a yell for AU and victory!

By: Martz/Murray, 1931
Arranged by: David Horne, 1999

Source of the words: Student Confederation.org Programming Spirit, Spirit Directors: Ali Lerner & Andy Resnick at: <wysiwyg://20/http://www. studentconfederation.org/events/spirit/>.

Chapter 1

Introduction

This book entails a pragmatic[1] analysis of the American University Alma Mater and Fight Song within a linguistic framework.[2] By delineating the pragmatic features of the songs, their symbolic[3] meanings are teased out. This is important because symbols, as some scholars have observed, are critical in promoting social integration, fostering legitimacy, inducing loyalty, gaining compliance, and providing citizens with security and hope (e.g., Edelman 1964, Jones 1964, Merelman 1966, Cobb and Elder 1976, Elder and Cobb 1983). These same factors must have motivated the University to post the songs on its Web site (http://www.american.edu/tour/songs/) accompanied by orchestral, a capella, orchestral with chorus, pep band, and swing music that can be listened to with an MP3 computer player. These factors must have also prompted the development of a Spirit Program (directed by Ali Lerner and Andy Resnick) with its Web site where the lyrics of the songs can be found (wysiwyg://20/http://www.studentconfederation.org/events/spirit/).

Also, an examination of the songs' texts clearly shows that the songs, like other textual symbols, convey not only surface contents, but a great deal of auxiliary contents as well. Thus, the major thesis in this book is the following: Analyses of school songs or other textual symbols that fail to account for pragmatic features risk ignoring relevant contents that may be central to the texts' meanings.

Consequently, this book is also about the possibility that significant *functional* explanations of textual symbols can be evaluated using linguistic features. The essence of an approach of this nature was captured by Stephen Levinson when he suggested the following:

> Most recent linguistic explanations have tended to be internal to linguistic theory: that is to say, some linguistic feature is explained by reference to other linguistic features, or to aspects of the theory itself. But there is another possible kind of explanation, often more powerful, in which some linguistic feature is motivated by principles outside the scope of linguistic theory (1983:40).

Thus, by employing pragmatic approaches to analyze the American University Alma Mater and Fight Song, the ideas underlying the songs' texts can be illuminated. This is possible because in the study of linguistic texts, as in the study of physics, special instruments, formulae, and laboratories beyond the grasp of the uninitiated can be utilized. Because one trained in linguistics possesses analytical skills and tools, and concepts that permit insights into the nature of language in general, s/he is in a better position than other analysts to explain the formal linguistic structures which constitute cues as to how the writers intended the songs to be interpreted.

Thus, the major questions probed in this book are the following: (1) What salient pragmatic features are imbedded in the texts of the American University Alma Mater and Fight Song? (2) How can the delineated pragmatic features be explained? In exploring these questions, the systematic application of discovery procedures well known in linguistic pragmatics will help to uncover propositions that will illuminate the texts examined for current readers.

American University: A Brief Background

American University is an 84-acre, independent, co-educational campus in a quiet neighborhood of Northwest Washington, DC (the relatively wealthier and safer section of the Nation's Capital). It has a student population of approximately 11,000, coming from all 50 states and more than 140 foreign countries. The university is divided into six undergraduate/graduate/professional Colleges/Schools: College of Arts and Sciences, Washington College of Law, Kogod School of Business, School of Communication, School of International Service, and School of Public Affairs. Its 2001-2002 freshman class's high school grade point average is 3.23, and its combined "recentered" average Scholastic Aptitude Test score is 1210. It has 566 full-time faculty members, with 90 percent of them holding advanced, academic degrees in their fields. The university has an average class size of 19 students and a student-faculty ratio of 14:1. It maintains varsity teams in golf, cross country, women's volleyball, lacrosse, field hockey, cheerleading, women's bas-ketball, men's basketball, women's soccer, men's soccer, track and field, and wrestling (http://www.american.edu/about/).

Although there has not been an abundance of literature on the history of American University, it is certain that the university has been a key player in many events in the history of the United States. Since its inception in 1898, American University has been intimately involved in the politics of this nation. Its location in Washington DC has promoted many relationships with presidents, vice presidents, several branches of the United States' government, and many key decision-makers in world politics. By using the nation's capital as a classroom, American University is able to offer a variety of unique experiences to students, as well as foster relationships that have helped the university grow into an experiential classroom.

American University founder, Bishop John Fletcher Hurst, was a member of the Methodist Board of Trustees in 1886 and had heard several leaders of Methodism express the desire for "an erection and endowment of a post graduate university at Washington" (Reynolds 1976: 10). Along with Theodore W. Tallmadge, Hurst began to search for a site for the new university; and after less than one month, they found it:

> The vision…came, as they rode along Loughboro Road, on the Northwestern Heights, a diversified and beautiful piece of ground. It was known as 'Bellevue,' ninety acres in extent, commanding a panoramic view over the District, the Manassas Plains, and the Blue Ridge Mountains of Western Maryland (Reynolds 1976: 13).

The real estate deal was finalized on January 24, 1890, when Hurst signed the papers claiming financial responsibility. He spent the next few months raising money and shoring up support for the university. By March 1, he and Reverend Charles W. Baldwin had raised $22,000, but his work was not finished (Reynolds 1976: 13).

In May 1892, "the General Conference of the Methodist Episcopal Church…approved The American University 'with the proviso that endorsements be secured of not less than five million dollars over and above its present real estate before opening for instruction'" (Reynolds 1976: 16). In 1893, the university was chartered by an Act of Congress; and in 1896, Bishop Hurst broke ground for the College of History, now known as Hurst Hall. According to Albert Osborn, from 1889-1902, the time of Bishop Hurst's resignation, Hurst had raised $400,000 in cash and $100,000 in property for the university (Reynolds 1976: vii). "At the time of his resignation in 1902, the total of the assets of the university was about two million dollars, the value of the 90-acre site having increased from $125,000 to $900,000" (Reynolds 1976: 16). Although Bishop Hurst had resigned from the university, he maintained his involvement in some university matters. He also continued his practice of traveling to Europe, as well as his quest for knowledge through scholarship, publications, and preaching, until his death on May 4, 1903 (Reynolds 1976: 20).

Throughout its history, American University would not be a stranger to those with political influence, and the tradition started on May 27, 1914 when President Woodrow Wilson addressed a gathering of people for the opening ceremonies of The American University. The *University Courier* reported:

> A cloudless day had wrapped in beauty the noble westward slope whereon lies the great university campus. On one side below was the national capital; its snowy buildings framed with green. Around the foot of the slope toward the south and east rolled the Potomac in a picturesque sweep toward the sea. The distant vista was of blue stretching mountains¼ It was to be an open-air assembly. Long before the hour set for the formal exercises the people had been gathering. Automobiles had been rolling out over Massachusetts Avenue boulevard. The new electric railroad, which had been complete for this special day, had brought visitors in a steady stream...(Reynolds 1976: 22).

This year (1914) saw the admission of the first class of American University graduate students; out of the twenty-eight students in all, four were women. The first class graduated in 1916, but the undergraduate program would not come into existence for over a decade.

On April 6, 1917, just three years after the opening of the university, the United States declared war on Germany; and before the end of the month, "Judge B.F. Leighton, president of the university's Board of Trustees, offered the use of the 90-acre campus and facilities for the war effort" (Reynolds 1976: 25). President Wilson accepted Judge Leighton's offer and the campus was turned into Camp American University and Camp Leach, a training ground for an estimated 100,000 troops (Reynolds 1976: 25). Due to the decreased availability of space, many classes were held in government and private buildings, as well as in homes of the instructors. By the end of World War I, the university purchased three properties on F Street in Northwest Washington, DC, in order to accommodate students from the government agencies who wished to attend graduate school.

In the fall of 1925, the university opened the College of Liberal Arts, as well as the first undergraduate program, in which seventy-five students were enrolled. This was also the year that *The American Eagle* was first published, and the first Women's Residence Hall was opened. As John Reynolds wrote, "The first year for the first students in the new college was a year of firsts—first football games, first dance, first intercollegiate debate, fist student newspaper, first dramatics production" (Reynolds 1976: 36). And in 1927, the first undergraduate class graduated from the College of Liberal Arts. This first undergraduate class of seventy-five boasted students from nineteen states and two foreign countries (Reynolds 1976: 36), a tradition American University still upholds. American University was also one of the first universities in a segregated city to admit black students.

However, tough times were ahead for American University. In 1939, the university lost its Middle States Association of Colleges and Secondary Schools (MSACSS) accreditation. After proposals for several internal changes were made and adopted, including the creation of the School of Public Affairs, MSACSS reinstated the university's accreditation.

At this time, the university was comprised of the School of Social Science and Public Affairs, the College of Arts and Sciences, and the Lucy Webb School of Nursing. From the 1920s, the university grew into an institution of 4,000, with enrollments increasing by over three thousand in an eleven-year period (Reynolds 1976: 49). According John R. Reynolds, the university was booming for several reasons:

> Scholars from European institutions were fleeing to America
> from the spread of war and despotism. Many area high school

graduates entered local universities and colleges because they could not afford to go away to college as a result of the economic depression. New Deal government employees working in expanding government agencies were badly in need of training (Reynolds 1976: 50).

In December 1941, the country became embroiled in another war; and once again, American University offered its facilities to aid in the war effort. "The university, for a second time in less than 25 years, was turned over to war-related activities" (Reynolds 1976: 57).

> Campus buildings were offered to, among others, the Committee for the Organization of World Peace, the C&P Telephone Company Training Center, the American Statistical Society, the American National Red Cross, the Armed Forces Institute editorial office, a local draft board headquarters, the SPARS, the U.S. Navy Bomb Disposal School, and the WAVES, who built a dormitory for over 2,000 WAVES in 1943 (Reynolds 1976: 57).

John R. Reynolds noted the following important developments at the university in the years after the war:

1946: The Business and Industrial Management undergraduate program was established; this was the predecessor of today's Kogod School of Business.

1947: WAMU, the university's radio station, was installed on campus; the Washington Semester Program was established.

1949: The Washington College of Law and American University decided to merge the two institutions (Reynolds 1976: 60).

From 1951 to 1967 (the "Anderson years"), Hurst Robins Anderson was the president of "the institution that was founded by his namesake, Bishop John Fletcher Hurst" (Reynolds 1976: 68). During these years, Anderson was responsible for the major growth witnessed by American University: in 1951, student enrollment was 6,291 and in 1967 it had increased to 14,770 (Reynolds 1976: 68). Anderson was also responsible for the major financial turnaround that American University underwent during the same years. When he began his term, the university had an operating deficit of $250,000. In the mid-1960's, the university also began to develop a "much closer" relationship with the United Methodist Church; Anderson worked to obtain funds for the founding of the School of International Service for which the university received one million dollars for the construction of the building in 1957. And just one year later, there was a groundbreaking ceremony for Wesley Theological Seminary.

In 1968, "students held rallies and 'teach-ins' on the steps of Mary Graydon Center on every subject ranging from the Vietnam War to the Columbia University riots and the Poor People's Campaign. Sixteen university students had been arrested for marijuana possession" (Reynolds 1976: 76). Students had drawn up a list of 12 demands that called for a confrontation with university administrators, who met with the students and, as a result, set up a conference of students, faculty, and administration. In the end, most of the students' demands were addressed, and Norman Cousins in the *Saturday Review* praised the university for its willingness to "meet with students and work out problems, and for avoiding the kind of violent protests that had been occurring at other colleges and universities" (Reynolds 1976: 76).

In October 1968, George H. Williams was elected president; he was the first non-Methodist president at American University. His goals were to "build even greater academic strengths and still maintain financial viability" (Reynolds 1976: 78). But in 1970, student unrest once again prevailed; upon hearing the news of the Kent State shootings, students voted to shut down the university; and the next day, the Student Senate endorsed the strikes. In the two days that followed, about 1,000 students from American University and surrounding universities and high schools protested and distributed leaflets in Ward Circle. Soon, the Metropolitan Police Department came to force the students back onto campus; the action resulted in an escalation in which students threw objects at the police who responded with tear gas. President Williams decided that the university would not close down (Reynolds 1976: 78). In a letter to students' parents, he wrote: "There is no reason for this university to be closed or for classes to be cancelled. We are an educational institution, and if rational discussions are to be achieved in a disrupted society, the colleges and universities must lead the way..." (Reynolds 1976: 78).

During his term as president, Williams also launched a 10 million-dollar campaign to construct a new library, one that would house an additional 600,000 volumes and increase student-seating capacity by 2,000 (Reynolds 1976: 81). However, in the two years of this campaign, the university could only manage to raise $2.2 million (Reynolds 1976: 83). In addition to the lack of funding for a new library, the then Provost Robert E. Cleary announced in September 1972 that there was a $6000,000 budget shortfall, a result of over three hundred students failing to return to the university (Arnold and Ross n.d.: VIII, 13). Around this same time, support from the United Methodist Church began to wane as the country had other, more pressing issues with which to contend (Arnold and Ross n.d.: VIII, 13).

Although the university was going through difficult financial times, Williams was able to address other needs of the university; among them, the establishment of the College of Public Affairs in 1972 and the School of Education in 1974, as well as various departments and other programs. "In all, the university developed 50 new programs from 1968 to 1975 and classes taught on campus increased by 12 per cent. The overall average class size decreased 25 per cent..." (Reynolds 1976: 83).

President Williams resigned in 1975 after suffering a heart attack, and Robert E. Cleary was appointed acting president.

During his short time as acting president, Cleary addressed many of the problems the university was facing, especially the library. Cleary was responsible for revising the original library plans, which called for the building to be mostly underground and proposed a "more practical and less expensive modular approach" (Arnold and Ross n.d.: VIII, 15). The Board of Trustees decided that the final plans would depend upon the amount of money available (Arnold and Ross n.d.: VIII, 15).

In October 1976, Dr. Joseph J. Sisco, the State Department's under-secretary for political affairs, was inaugurated as the president of American University (Arnold and Ross n.d.: VIII, 15-16). Sisco agreed with the Board of Trustees' new plan for building the library, and the groundbreaking took place in the spring of 1977 and was formally dedicated as the Jack I. and Dorothy G. Bender Library and Learning Resources Center on April 21, 1979 (Arnold and Ross n.d.: VIII, 18). In the first year of Sisco's term, the university received unprecedented gifts in excess of $1.4 million (Arnold and Ross n.d.: VIII, 18). Sisco's desire to be involved in public life and foreign affairs eventually led to his resignation as the president of American University in 1980, at which time Dr. Richard Berendzen, a well respected Physics professor specializing in Astronomy, was elected American University's eleventh president (Arnold and Ross n.d.: VIII, 20).

Unfortunately, that fall semester started out less promising than past semesters. "Fewer high school seniors and the university's increased admission standards resulted in a decline of 5% in total enrollments" (Arnold and Ross n.d.: IX, 7). Over the next few years, major administrative changes were made; it was predicted that enrollment would continue to decline, and tuition was scheduled to increase by almost 13% (Arnold and Ross n.d.: IX, 9). However, by 1984, things were starting to turn around again for the university: the fiscal year ended with a surplus, university endowments were at the highest level in history, and freshman applications were up by 10% (Arnold and Ross n.d.: IX, 10).

In 1986, the university established the Office of Minority Affairs; and in 1987, it began to phase out the School of Nursing. The spring 1988 commencement was the first to be held in the new Adnan Khashoggi Sports and Convocation Center. "The decade came to an encouraging end as the District of Columbia Board of Zoning Adjustments approved the university's master plan for the campus for the years 1989-2000" (Arnold and Ross n.d.: IX, 18).

Although the new decade began full of hope, the next year was difficult for the university. Richard Berendzen resigned as president of the university. "Provost Greenberg called the campus together, acknowledged the difficult time the university was experiencing [and] encouraged everyone to work together" (Arnold and Ross n.d.: X, 3). During this time, Greenberg was appointed Interim President. However, it was this same year that Eric A. Friedheim donated $1 million for a new arts facility, the Eric A. Friedheim Quandrangle was named, and Dr. Joseph Duffey became the twelfth president. Also, "The Society of Professional Journalists announced that it had selected *The Eagle* the best all-around, non-daily student newspaper in the country" (Arnold and Ross n.d.: X, 6).

In 1993, President Clinton named Duffey Director of the United States Information Agency and Duffey resigned his presidency "with deep regret" (Arnold and Ross n.d.: X, 7). Elliott Milstein became the Interim President until Benjamin Ladner was named the thirteenth President of American University in March 1994.

One of the many elements that make American University's history so colorful and unique is its involvement with prominent United States figures. Since 1898, American University has had the honor of receiving some of the nation's most eminent people. Among those who have contributed to the character of American University are several presidents, beginning with President William McKinley, who accepted an invitation to serve on the Board of Trustees. President Theodore Roosevelt, also a member of the Board of Trustees, laid the cornerstone for the McKinley Building in place of President McKinley who was assassinated in 1901. The building was originally to be named for McKinley's home state of Ohio, but the name was changed to honor the late president.

Woodrow Wilson also spoke at American University's official opening on May 27, 1914. He again visited the university in November 1917 to inspect the facilities after the university offered its campus to the war effort. President Warren G. Harding spoke at the commencement in 1921 and served on the university's Board of Trustees from 1920 until his death in 1923. In 1934, Franklin D. Roosevelt was the first president to receive an honorary degree from the university. Although Herbert C. Hoover was also scheduled to receive an honorary degree, he did not as he was unable to attend the commencement ceremonies. He did, however, serve on the Board of Trustees form 1945 to 1950, and then as an honorary trustee from 1950 to1964. Harry S. Truman was also an honorary trustee form 1959 to 1972 and "received, at the White House Oval Office, participants of the Summer Institute for Teachers of American Government, held by AU in cooperation with the American Political Science Association in 1948" (*American University Alumni Directory* 1999:xviii).

In 1957, Dwight D. Eisenhower was the keynote speaker at the groundbreaking ceremonies for the School of International Service where he also received an honorary degree; Eisenhower was an honorary trustee from 1961 to 1969. The university was also fortunate enough to receive President John F. Kennedy as the speaker for commencement in 1963, in which he announced a major foreign policy decision:

> Premier Nakita Kruschev and British Prime Minister Harold McMillan and he had agreed to begin decisions about a

comprehensive test ban treaty. And second, that the United States does not propose to conduct nuclear tests in the atmosphere as long as other states do not do so (Reynolds 1976: 73).

American University President Hurst Anderson also awarded President Kennedy an honorary degree during that ceremony.

In addition to United States presidents, American University has also welcomed speakers such as Former President Gerald R. Ford, Vice President Hubert H. Humphrey, former president of Zimbabwe, Canaan Banana, Muhammed Ali, Jack Valenti, Dalai Lama, novelists Chinua Achebe (Nobel Laureate) and Ariel Dorfman, Former First Ladies Barbara Bush and Rosslyn Carter, former Israeli Prime Minister Shimon Peres, former Israeli Foreign Minister Abba Eban, Washington D.C. Mayor Anthony Williams, novelist-in-hiding Salman Rushdie, and National Public Radio journalist Daniel Schorr.

Basic Organization of the Rest of the Book

The following chapter (two) discusses various theoretical postulates on meaning, since the essence of this book is to tease out the linguistic pragmatic meanings in the texts of the American University Alma Mater and Fight Song. The chapters after that (three, four, five, six, and seven) entail discussions of the historical context, deixis, presuppositions, implicatures, and speech acts of the texts, respectively. In each of these chapters, the pertinent concept is defined and its scope clearly delimited in terms of the texts studied. The final chapter (eighth) draws conclusions based on the findings.

The texts studied in this book comprise a closed set of statements within which it is easier to guess how and why new insights emerged, and what was overlooked. Occasionally, they show 'new' ideas are rediscoveries. But since today's studies about symbolic texts are in process, to understand them, let alone to evaluate them, is more difficult. Analysts abandon or redefine traditional terms, and produce such a welter of innovations, that it is not easy to find a neutral framework within which they can be compared.

What unifies the chapters in this book can appear rather banal. But many linguistic insights are so obvious, so fundamental, that they are difficult to absorb, appreciate, and express with fresh clarity. Some of the more basic ones will be isolated from accounts of investigators who have earned their contemporaries' respect. Thus, the originality of this book hinges upon the clarity with which familiar but unconnected facts about the texts analyzed are marshaled into a simpler, linguistically satisfying unity.

Endnotes

1. Linguistic pragmatics has been generally defined by Stephen Levinson as "the study of language usage" (1983:5).

The subject matter of this book is pragmatics—an approach that is attributable to language philosopher Charles Morris (1938), who sought to outline the general shape of a science of signs, or *Semiotics*. In its essence, pragmatics is the study of meaning from the point of view of language users, especially of the choices they make, the constraints they encounter in using language in social interactions, and the effects their uses of language have on other participants in an act of communication. The study of pragmatics can be divided into two major categories: (1) *Applied Pragmatics* deals with verbal interactions in such domains as medical interviews, language teaching, judicial sessions, etc., where problems of communication are vital; (2) *General Pragmatics* deals with the principles governing the communicative uses of language, especially as encountered in conversations.

What pragmaticists cover has become so enormous that to discuss all that goes under the rubric of pragmatics in dealing with two relatively short texts (the American University Alma Mater and Fight Song) is neither possible nor desirable. As such, this book considers only the main topics in the Anglo-American linguistic tradition that builds directly, for the most part, on philosophical approaches to language of both logic and ordinary language variety. These topics include: speech acts, deixis, presupposition, and implicature. A fifth topic is conversational structure, which is not dealt with in this book simply because the songs studied are not conversational texts.

The alternative approach is called the continental tradition. This approach is broader and includes much that is subsumed under the rubric of *Sociolinguistics*—a discipline that investigates the relationship between language and society.

2. The term linguistic framework as used here refers to a way of studying various aspects of human language and its interaction with other areas of human culture and behavior, which calls for collecting pertinent data concerning a range of linguistic phenomena, observing the patterns which underlie those phenomena, and expressing the observed regularities by means of certain linguistic rules.

3. According to Roger Cobb and Charles Elder, "A symbol is any object used by human beings to index meanings that are not inherent in, nor discernible from, the object itself" (1983:28).

Chapter 2

On Meaning

This chapter seeks to integrate several sociolinguistic approaches to *meaning* into a synthesis of what underlies them all as a background for understanding the pragmatic meanings in the American University Alma Mater and Fight Song. While natural scientists share data which are objectively testable on public criteria, sociolinguists appear to lack such data. The approaches to *meaning* (a label for what 'semantics' and 'pragmatics' have in common) lack a shared clarity. No study provides an incontrovertible basis for defining *meaning*. So, 'sociolinguistic' conclusions appear to be contrary. That leads to an enormous waste of scholarly effort and conflicting results, with the consequence that funding agencies may view the effort as inherently inconclusive. It also generates few acceptable answers to guide the student of linguistics.

A summary which may isolate universal principles and identify particular parameters is, therefore, important. But it suggests that no matter how refined and how elaborate the analysis, it will still be a structure on shifting sand.

This chapter, thus, attempts to build a theory of how to analyze some approaches to *meaning* used by sociolinguists by summarizing their results and methods. The test of such theory is whether or not it explains what is commonly accepted as certain (of course, no such result appears in this version).

This effort is relevant to epistemological disputes about the justification of induction. Kaplan (1974:20) recalled Hume's idea that pattern-persistence is neither a projection of a tautology nor the outcome of experiential evidence. So this chapter will examine sequentially (1) semantic versus pragmatic perspectives on meaning, (2) three philosophical levels of meaning, (3) directness versus indirectness, and (4) natural versus non-natural meaning.

Semantic Versus Pragmatic Perspectives on Meaning

Comparable perspectives which led to distinguishing *langue* and *parole* motivate drawing a boundary between *semantics* and *pragmatics*[1]–the contrast between *mean* in

(1) What did the professor *mean* by ONOMA?

(2) What does ONOMA *mean*?[2]

Pragmatics assumes that an acceptable answer to these questions is based on the image of *meaning* as a polyadic relation among conventionality-speaker-situation-hearer; *semantics*, a triadic relation between conventionality, language and to what it refers. The latter, as refined by Morris (1938, 1946) or Carnap (1942), ignores pragmaticists' insistence on speech-situational determinants. Perhaps *mean* in (1) and (2) is the concern of both disciplines. Both contrast with Leech's assumption that "semantics traditionally deals with meaning as a dyadic relation,…while pragmatics deals with meaning as a triadic relation…" (1983:6). For only if language were natural could *meaning* be dyadic; conventionality makes it triadic; pragmatics must be polyadic. And defining *meaning* exhaustively in terms of reference may exclude a semantic study of morphological affixes and syntactic constructions.

Imprecise terminology makes it difficult to distinguish the focus of Semantics and Pragmatics. This may be because psychologically, *meaning* is context, but logically and metaphysically, *meaning* is much more than psychological context; or put differently, whatever *meaning* may be, psychology is concerned with it only so far as it can be represented in terms of contextual imagery.

Pragmatics lacks a single model which locates it precisely within a general theory of communication dominating a sub-theory of verbal communication. This does not render pragmatics useless, however. For models have presuppositions and shortcomings: the Porphyrian Tree 'models' what a primitive term entails; Transformational Grammar takes 'S' as a primitive; but is 'communicative' a primitive term? One would hope not.

Gazdar's (1979) model defines Communication as encoding and decoding; his (sub)model of Pragmatics defines that discipline as application of an arbitrary set of rules to sentence- and context-descriptions to produce utterance-interpretations. As he put it, "pragmatics has as its topic those aspects of the meaning of utterances which cannot be accounted for by straightforward reference to truth conditions of the sentences uttered" (1979:2-3).

Grcie's (1975) model interprets sentences as speakers' attempts to be truthful, informative, relevant and clear, paired with hearers' evaluation of speakers' success. In essence, people are constantly trying to maintain certain standards in their communicative behavior.

Gazdar's code model makes hearer-evaluation arbitrary; Grice's makes it motivated because of shared knowledge, rules and maxims. The main difference between the two models, therefore, lies within the level of generality at which they approach the facts of verbal communication.

These two ways of taking communication theory admits semantics as code, but not pragmatics—code would come under syntax or phonetics, while pragmatics involves extra-code abilities. So semantics includes *meaning-change*, logical validity and linguistic relativity (based on the data presented earlier).

Morris labeled sign-sign relations *syntactics*; sign-behavior relations *pragmatics*, and sign-world relations *semantics*: the whole is *semiotic*. Semiotics, then, is conceived as the general theory of signs.

This distinction of semantics and syntax impoverishes Semantics and overloads the purview of Pragmatics with whatever does not yield to a truth-value calculus. Linguistics exclude from Semantics what most interests 'semanticists.' Thus, it is obvious that (1) *naming* is basic; that (2) we cannot communicate about that for which we lack *names*; that (3) *sentence-meaning* is a function of prior *word-meaning*; and (4) words in or out of context–sentential or other–still have signification.

It is true that not all words have semantic *meaning* (e.g., proper names in Western languages do not; operators have only syntactic *meaning*). So Semantics is, as Whorf (1956:213-252) and Taylor (1971:24) suggested, (the study of) languages (which) constitute (their own unique) realities.[3]

Three Levels of Meaning

Harman (1968:590-602) gives three ways philosophers approach *meaning*[4]: (I) Ayer, Lewis, J. R. Firth, Hempel, Sellars, Quine, etc. focus on *meaning's* connection with evidence for inference: how words function in speakers' 'language game.' "Game" glosses ove a lot: Ayer pits empirical against other kinds of evidence; Lewis, common versus mutual knowledge; Hempel, statistical versus actual expectation; J. R. Firth, social versus cognitive purposes; Sellars, categorization versus motivation; Quine, analytic versus syntactic *meaning* (Herman's 1989 [1986] mentions these and others).

(II) Morris, Stevenson, Grice and Katz, etc. put the *meaning* of an expression in the idea, thought, feeling, or emotion it can communicate: that is, how hearers re-encode speakers' words into ideas, etc.

These authors, however, differ radically about the + or -physical reality of 'ideas,' etc. and about the legitimacy of non-empirical 'evidence.'

(III) Austin, Hare, Nowell-Smith, Searle amd Alston, etc. take *meaning* to concern the speech acts expressions can perform. 'Speech-activists,' though, stress subjective intention versus objective possibilities.

A II-type theory of communication presupposes a I-type (defining thought); III-types mostly presupposes a II-type: to order someone to do something, one must communicate what is to be done (Harman 1968:592). Explanations of these theories and objections to them ensue.

I-types explain what it is to think-believe-desire X, as though such processes all demand language, natural or other, that is coherent if speaker's thought relies on a language. Non-speakers may well think-believe-desire X exquisitely, but be unable to communicate what they have experienced without language. Human language is a communication-tool that can be put to many uses for which it is not eminently best designed. If that language is unknown, it is described in the investigator's linguistic terms.

All (I- II- and III-types) ignore the social aspects of language and concentrate on the inferential. Private languages preventing communication are deemed possible. Besides, evidentiality presupposes intersubjective agreement about its objectivity, which presupposes communication about what makes evidence evident, while neglecting to deal with *meaning* in communication (Harman 1968:590).

Some language-uses do not require appeal to evidence, as in asking 'What is your name?' It is not appropriate to look for the evidence for what has been said.

II-theories are like Katz's (1966:98) postulate that to 'understand' what A says is to match A's code with one's own. 'Code-sharing' is another way of saying that language is conventional, not natural, and that to share a language is to share that convention.

Harman found Katz's postulate circular when applied to words—that speakers' thought-words are identical with those which speakers and hearers both use in speech. But only the literal-minded types Harman mocks could confuse logical, poetic and rhetorical usage, distinguished since antiquity.

Another postulate is Grice's (1957):

> Speaker *means-nn* (part of a private language preventing communication) z by uttering U iff:
> (i)   S intended U to cause some effect z in recipient H
> (ii) S intended (i) to be achieved simply by H recognizing that intention (i)
> where z = a belief or volition invoked in H
>   (paraphrased by Levinson 1983:16).

Harman found this equally circular in that it eliminates simple communicative intent in favor of speech acts. Promising, for example, does more than communicate intent; asking someone to do something is to more than communicate a desire that he does it (1968:67).

Harman appears to have ignored Grice's insight that what S *means* by U is not necessarily related to U's *meaning* (one would hope that Harman was aware of this truism)—if U has a conventional one at all: 'The professor was quite interesting' may be ironic, conveying the opposite.

III-theories take *meaning* as speech-act potentials. Alston (1964:36ff) equated *same-meaning* with same-illocutionary potential: expressions have the same *meaning* only if they can implement the same illocutionary acts.

Harman found that circular as well. He said that either 'Pass the water' or Pass the H_2O' to implement the same speech act can only be evaluated by deciding that this pair have the same *meaning*.[5]

More importantly, that example ignores Chomsky's (1964:57) language 'creativity': i.e. language is for *free* expression of thought; what uses are made of language comes second. (This expression is novel, but the insight is as old as Western civilization.)

In short, Harman found Katz and Fodor to believe that an adequate semantic theory shows *sentence-meaning* as determined by lexical *meaning* and grammatical structure. They did not bother to set up a theory of how speakers use the language in which they think. However, it can be argued that Katz and Fodor believed that a theory of competence is adequate for their purposes and that it is not a theory of performance: others are, thus, free to handle the latter.

For example, Artificial Intelligence (AI) translates ordinary language into explicit representations which computers can use to elicit intelligent responses. Difficulties show how important covert knowledge versus overt expression is (for example, see Charniak 1972 f). Computers only work on what is actually in them—what Saussure labeled 'relations among things present'—overt syntagmatics. Humans register present things against 'relations among things absent'—covert paradigmatics. *The Washington Post* (February 05, 1990), for example, sketched Searle's Chinese-label test for AI attempts to simulate human exchanges in English: what both have in common is overt; what machines lack is covert—called consciousness or parallel awareness.

Harman was puzzled by Chomsky's claim that one 'knowing' a language 'knows' its grammatical rules, since s/he would attribute the latter only to grammarians, not ordinary speakers (1968:74). This may be the case in 1968, but no longer. We now readily grasp how people can 'know' things *consciously*, or *subconsciously*, or *unconsciously*.

All this suggests that Pragmatics is concerned with context, not linguistic competence as defined by Chomsky's syntax or Katz's lexicon. To account for non-referring-items like *well* and *oh* is beyond syntax as defined in Transformational Grammar (TG) and better handled pragmatically as indicating concerns like *relevance implicature* or *discourse structure.* Competence-model grammars must refer to pragmatic information or fail to account fully for the lexical items of a language.

Directness Versus Indirectness

Austin (1962) and Searle (1969, 1976 and 1985), as discussed further in Chapter 7, show the amount of work involved in interpretation parallels + or -directness. In order to delineate 'direct' speech act, one assumes a context-free situation where:

(1) S wants H to do X,
(2) so S says 'Do X' to H, and
(3) H interprets S wants H to do X.

A speech act is 'direct' when H needs no more than S's utterance to enable H to identify S's intention with her/his words. Saying 'Sorry about coming late to class' can directly express a psychological state.[6] If S's goal is to *apologize*, there is no intention to *claim* to be, nor an aim at *being late*. The expression's content must be equally shared by speaker and hearer as follows:

Literal Meaning $\rightarrow$ Content $\rightarrow$ Speaker's Meaning

where literal meaning determines content which, in turn, determines speaker's meaning.

Hence, the following assumptions:

(1) Directness does not usually create ambiguity.
(2) Directness results from a single speech act.
(3) Directness produces acts whose literal meaning exhausts illocutionary force.[7]

In the simplest direct case, speakers choose a clear and literal match of intention and expression and the hearer accepts it as such on the basis of ordinary language conventions.

Searle found that the following *felicity conditions* are required for an 'indirect directive':

(1) Preparatory:	H must be capable of performing A
(2) Sincerity:	S really wants H to do A
(3) Propositional Content:	S predicates[8] a future act A of H
(4) Essential:	Counts as an attempt by S to get H to do A

Interpreting indirects is the opposite of interpreting directs (except for idioms). So 'Can you tell me the meaning in Temne (a language of Sierra Leone)?' merits a double interpretation: as a *question* or a *request* that H do something, diagrammable as follows:

$$\rightarrow \text{ Speaker's Meaning 1}$$
$$\text{Literal Meaning} \rightarrow \text{Context}$$
$$\rightarrow \text{ Speaker's Meaning 2}$$

where literal meaning determines context which, in turn, determines speaker's meanings.

Thus, the following assumptions:

(1) Indirectness creates ambiguity.
(2) Indirectness entails two speech acts.
(3) Indirectness entails acts whose literal meanings do not exhaust illocutionary force.

The problem, then, is the following: How can S use a single expression with two *meanings* and intend H to grasp both? Intentions are private,[9] utterances are public.[10] How can H distinguish between ambiguities in utterances? Some ambiguities are all but eliminated by convention: 'Can to pass the salt?' is a good example (Searle 1975:60).

Searle, therefore, defined indirects as 'cases where one illocutionary act is performed indirectly by way of performing another.' So an indirect is a means of performing a direct speech act.

So even direct imperatives, for example, 'Turn on the light!', can be indirect, given a further goal, and 'indirect' becomes a matter of degree, lending itself to an analysis of the *length* of a means-to-end-chain. Definitions using the term to be defined makes sense only to one who already understands that term: *direct* and *indirect* define each other by contrast. An autonomous definition for either is clearly needed.

In essence, both directness and indirectness rest on H's ability, future actions and desire or willingness versus those of S. S's *meaning-differences* resulting in + or -directness depend on H's perception of S's intentions. This describes the + or -direct situation superficially. It definitely does not explain how options are limited nor how H distinguishes between them.

Natural Versus Non-natural Meaning (*Meaning-nn*)

To keep natural[11] and non-natural (Intentional: *mean-nn*) transfer of information distinct, and divide incidental from 'proper' communication, Grice noted these senses for *mean-nn* (1975:55-56):

(a) x meantNN something (on a particular occasion) and
(b) x meantNN that so-and-so (on a particular occasion)[12]
(c) A meantNN something by x (on a particular occasion)
(d) A meantNN by x that so-and-so (on a particular occasion)[13]

to help make clearer

(e) x meansNN (timeless) something (that so-and-so)[14]
(f) A meansNN (timeless) by x something (that so-and-so)[15]

with each expression explicated (Grice 1975:58):

(c) <-> 'A intended the utterance x to produce some effect in an audience by means of the recognition of the intention.' To ask what A meant is to ask for a specification of the intended effect (though one cannot always get a straightforward 'a belief that...' reply).

(b) <-> 'Somebody meantNN something by x' but it does not always work.

(e <-> some statement or disjunction of statements about 'what people intend ('recognition' qualified) to be affected by x...'

Levinson (1983:16) found Grice's meanNN definition to be opaque at first, then that it reduces to saying communication consists of a Speaker intending to cause a Hearer to think or do something merely by getting H to recognize S is trying to cause that thought or action. *Communication*, thus, is a complex intention, the goal of which is achieved or satisfied by being recognized.[16] For Levinson, communication entails mutuality: S knows that H knows...that S has a specific communicative intention (if communication is successful).

For example, (i) I say what I know will make you angry and I succeed: I have used 'natural' means.[17] (ii) If you know that I am always mouthing things like that, I may or may not succeed: if it works, only (ii) is communication (meanNN) in Grice's sense, and it includes non-verbal means.[18]

Ziff (1967:61) sniffed that Grice's account can turn nonsense into sense.[19] For example, George, inducted into the army, had to take a sanity test. Deeming the test fit only for morons, George answers an officer's simple question with the following:

ugh ugh blugh blugh blugh ugh blugh blugh.

Grice must say that George meantNN something: he intended his utterance to produce an effect on H, since H would recognize that intent—to offend H. Since that offence was indeed George's primary intent, it fits Grice's requirements.

For Ziff, George both did meanNN something and did not *mean* anything by his utterance. So he found that Grice confounds speaker's and utterance *meaning*.

Ziff suggested that studying what an S might intend by using an expression is to study the expression's use that is multi-determined and can involve acoustic shape, length, or much else irrelevant to the expression's *meaning* (1967:64-65). (It is frustrating to find in Ziff's paper about *meaning* only that of *expression*, but not *sense, refer, infer, connote, imply, presuppose* and the like.)

Thus, Ziff concluded that Grice's analysis lack projective devices: "The semantic and syntactic structure of any language is essentially recursive in character. What any given sentence means depends on what (various) other sentences in the language mean" (Ziff 1967:65). This rewards Saussure's contention molded on the syntagmatic and paradigmatic axes, resulting in a form's *value* and *content*.

Indeed, Ziff missed how Grice's ideas are important to pragmatics, since they suggest how S-H-meaningNN and sentence meaning can diverge—as in ironic 'That's interesting!' A conventional degree of conversational 'implicitness' virtually insures that what S *means* is not exhausted by the sense of the forms uttered (cf. Levinson 1983:17-18 for more on this).

Grice's natural versus non-natural distinction, however, does not clarify the distinction between semantics and pragmatics. It just leaves pragmatics as an area of linguistics concerned with aspects of *meaning* not covered in semantics.

In sum, analyzing these analyses of *meaning* invoked by sociolinguists shows that neither *meaning* nor *meaning-models* nor *theories of meaning* define themselves. While concentration on one aspect of *meaning* may be appropriate for a seminar, scholarly work must reconcile as many as possible. How aspects long-discussed are modified by new insights clarifies the extent to which one or the other is in focus.

Indeed, models do not explain themselves any more than isolated terms. What both presuppose must be made overt, and what limits the elements of a model impose on model-interpretations must be made explicit.

Endnotes

1. *Langue* and *parole* contrast sociological and individual objects; *semantics* and *pragmatics* concern relations of either object.

2. *Mean's* lexical semantics are identical in the S-semantics of What did the professor *mean*? and What does ONOMA *mean*? (1) & (2) contrast syntactically as + or -transitive (VP → V NP vs VP → V), semantically as action [A, O, (E)] vs state [O, (E)]–pragmatically.

3. Another distinguishable generalization: unless English were capable of escaping the very limitation Whorf observed, he could not have communicated his revolutionary discovery and we could not grasp enough of what he was saying to agree or disagree with him.

4. Any one of these positions *defines* itself best by *not* being what the others are. More positions are possible, and each scholar listed has his own peculiar interest-focus.

Harman (1988:118) quoted Sellars (1963) on concept-use: "(1) the perceptual categorization of what one perceives, (2) the use of concepts in getting oneself to act in one way or another, and (3) the use of concepts in reasoning to get from some thoughts to others."

5. One would hope that Harman knew too much to have concluded that others excluded the defeasibility of alternate definitions of *meaning* when they focused on one of them.

6. Norms of frequency are taken for granted here. Taiwanese ask 'Have you eaten?' in circumstances where we say 'Hello' or 'How are you?' Both 'questions' may get detailed answers.

7. Chomsky (1959) noted the empirical vacuity of Behaviorists reciprocally defining stimulus and response: all three of these say a speech act is single and direct if unambiguous, otherwise it is indirect and multiple.

8. Strange use of the word *predicate*: predicates are classes to which subjects belong ('Jim is tall'), hence 'predicate logic.'

9. So one finds the expression *intended meaning* ambiguous between at least sense and reference.

10. Hence, the expression *conventional meaning* with the same refinements.

11. 'Signs' exclude two interpretations for normals all alone or in groups (dark clouds: storm) and resist change. 'Symbols' inherit interpretations stably for group-members but tolerate change variably (*beards* and *beard* & *corpulence* and *fat* in China).

12. Perhaps dividing the fixed history of (a) labels [like *homely*] from (b) assertions using a label [like *you're homely*–a likely insult in a United States situation, but more likely a compliment in a Great Britain one].

13. Perhaps distinguishing (c) a deliberate speaker's label-choice as (d) situationally appropriate to an assertion.

14. Confounds 'apt' label; (a) and '+ or -true' assertion (b); *timeless* is literally applicable only to natural, not non-natural *meaning*.

15. If A = S, this assertion seems to speak while ignoring label-instability and construction adaptability.

16. *-tion*-forms in English (*communication, intention*) are ambiguously stative, processive or active, so this terminology can confuse.

17. This evacuates the universal natural/non-natural dichotomy proposed earlier. A kick angers all, being called a son-of-a-bitch or a son-of-a-pig flatters few but evokes varied reactions in different cultures.

18. So we distinguish (i) an attempted insult—illocution from (ii) a potentially insulting expression from (iii) an insult—perlocution (by definition, a *successful* illocution) as well as the functional equivalence between some words and gestures.

19. This is a good example of *equivocation* (use of a single phonetic form with more than one unrelated interpretation) and the need to use as many specific terms for the generic *mean(ing)* as possible.

Chapter 3

Historical Context of the Alma Mater & Fight Song

The major purpose of this chapter is to discuss the historical context within which the currently used American University Alma Mater and Fight Song were written. It is anticipated that this context will provide some background information that will help to account for the types of pragmatic meanings embedded in the texts. Also briefly discussed are the other American University school songs. Before doing so, however, it makes sense to begin with a discussion of the essence of historical context.

The Role of Historical Context

According to David and Chava Nachmias (1981:87), the historical method involves the examination of related events occurring during the time the main event being studied took place. The strength of the historical method, as Babbie (1992:312) has pointed out, hinges on the fact that it is a qualitative approach employed to master many subtle details. The main sources for observation and analysis are historical records.

However, as Kaplan argued more than 30 years ago, "the historian does not provide us with a picture of the past, a representation of it 'as it really was' apart from any interpretations of his own; neither does any other scientist with respect to his subject matter" (1964:361). This is not to suggest, according to Kaplan, "that the historian must engage in the process of interpretation even to arrive at what are distinctively his data does not mean that his findings are doomed to subjectivity" (1964:361). Indeed, what the historian deals with is an affirmation about the event—an interpretation of an act as a certain act—that constitutes for the reader a historical fact.

In terms of textual analysis, Patterson suggested that the new interest in history stems from a polemic: "it derives its energy from a conviction that literary texts have always been, more or less, products of their historical, social, political, and economic environments and that they cannot be understood unless one attempts to resituate them within those conditions" (1992:185). Thus, it is the historicist's job to interpret texts in light of their original contexts.

Also, Hume identified four aspects of the historicist's enterprise in interpreting literary texts. These four aspects are: (1) the collection of new facts and primary materials, (2) the contextual interpretation of facts, (3) the application of context to text, and (4) making contexts from texts (1996:2). Going from text to context, according to Hume, "helps sensitize us to the original, the abnormal, the subversive" (1996:2).

Indeed, without the notion of *context*, there would be no theory of pragmatics. This is one reason pragmatics calls for some explicit characterization of the concept of context, despite the difficulty encompassed in such an activity. This truism is captured by Schiffrin when she posited that

> Discourse markers, contextualization cues, and sociolinguistic variables all have a contextualizing function. The markers are clues to the local contexts of utterances, contextualization cues to the interpretive schemas within which

communicative intent is situated, and sociolinguistic variables to the social and expressive meanings of self, other,
and situation. But because discourse markers are function-
ally linked to these other devices, the study of all these
devices together can provide an emic guideline to speakers'
contextualization of language at several different levels at
once (1987:30).

For ethnomethodologists in particular, the analyzability of actions in
context as a practical accomplishment is a must. As Garfinkel insisted,
this must be the case because "not only does no concept of context-in-
general exist, but every use of context without exception is itself essentially indexical" (1967:10). Ethnomethodologists are interested,
therefore, less in he contribution to the conversational system made by
the specific identities of the speakers and more in the contribution of
immediate conversational context.

As Heritage (1984:242) stated, the significance of a speaker's communicative action is doubly contextual in both *context-shaped*[1] and
context-renewing.[2] Furthermore, he suggested that while these aspects
of context are traceable to Garfinkel's notions of indexical and reflexive
characteristics of talk and action, they have also found some parallel
expression in Goffman's more enthnographically-oriented studies.

For Goffman (1974:496-497), context helps an analyst to rule out
unintended meanings and suppress misunderstandings.[3] And that the
immediate surrounding could not have this power apart from the cultural competence of interpreters. In addition, he noted that the correct
interpretation of any statement may have as one of its implications the
saving of the interpreter from exposure as someone who presumes cultural ad linguistic competence s/he does not possess.

This way of conceptualizing context can be thought of as a process
whereby the native speaker of a given language produces contextually
appropriate and internally coherent utterances—a process which

involves a lot more than knowledge of the language system. Thus, the factors identified by a system's framework as contextual must be those factors that determine the native speaker's production and interpretation of utterances in actual activities of use.

Another notion of context in Goffman's work (even though he did not call it so) is a *physical* one: the role of *setting* in performance. According to Goffman (1974:22), *setting* includes furniture, decor, physical layout, and other background items which provide the scenery and stage props for the spate of human action. *Setting* stays put, geographically speaking, so that those who use it as part of their performance cannot begin their act until they have brought themselves to the appropriate place and must end their performance upon their departure. Goffman's formulation of context is, indeed, pragmatic: It covers the identities of participants, the temporal and spatial parameters of speech events, the knowledge and metaknowledge, intentions and beliefs of the participants in those speech events. This makes context paramount in any discourse analysis.

Historical Context of the Alma Mater and the Fight Song

It was in 1931 that both the currently used American University Alma Mater was composed by John M. Houston and Clair S. Atland and the currently used American University Fight Song was composed by Martz/Murray (the latter is probably Louise Murray who wrote the music to the American University Pledge Song that appears in the 1930-1931 and 1931-1932 editions of the *American University Student Handbook*). Both songs were arranged by David Horne in 1999. While no additional information can be found on the original composers of these songs, there is plenty on David Horne. As a matter of fact, there is an Internet Web site that features Horne's biography and his work (http://www.davidhorne.fsnet. co.uk/maintext.html).

Horne was born in Scotland in 1970. He is currently a doctoral degree candidate at Harvard University in Boston, Massachusetts. He has appeared in piano recitals and concertos both in Europe and the United States. He has appeared with Alea III, Auros, Boston Music Viva, and other groups. He has received fellowships from Tanglewood and Marlboro and awards including a commission from the Koussevitsky Foundation for his work as a composer. His works have been commissioned and performed by international soloists and orchestras including Boris Beresovsky, Evelyn Glennie, Nobuko Imai, Fred Sherry, Ygdrassil String Quartet (of Stockholm, Sweden), the Scottish Chamber Orchestra, London Sinfonietta, and London Philharmonic. His music has also been performed by groups such as the California EAR Unit, The Fires of London, Mendelssohn String Quartet, Speculum Musicae, Orchestra 2001, Chamber Music Society of Lincoln Center, and Ensemble für Neue Musik Zurich. Several of Horne's works have been recorded, most recently by BMG/RCA. His recent commissions include an orchestral work toured in Australia and the United Kingdom by the Camerata Orchestra, a full length theater work, *Beyond the Blue Horizon*, performed by the British Sinfonia and Trestle Theater Company on a five-week tour of the United Kingdom, a vocal work for the British Broadcasting Service's Schubert Celebrations. His chamber opera, *Travelers*, has been premiered at London's Covent Garden Festival. His other premiers have included works commissioned by London's City Chamber Choir (from mezzo, choir and orchestra), the 1998 International Viola Congress, and the Portland Chamber Music Festival. Horne also has done a full-length opera that was commissioned by Scottish Opera for its 1999-2000 season (http://www.bmv.org/bios/david-horne.html).

The year 1931 during which the American University Alma mater and Fight Song were composed saw the University, like the rest of the United States, in the midst of the Great Depression. After the crash of 1929, the American economy began a dismal descent that lasted until

1933. The images of the era included 9,000 failed banks, a quarter of the labor for unemployed as millions were unable to find work, bread lines, tattered clothes, destitutes living in cardboard hovels, roads filled with vagabonds (Hughes and Cain 1994:444).

The following statistics vividly reflect the country's economic crisis between 1929 and 1932: manufacturing fell by half; railway passenger-car output fell from 2202 units to a mere 7; automobile production fell 75 percent—from 4.5 million to 1.1 million; hamburgers were two for five cents, but people could not afford them; people would work for 10 cents per hour, but employers could not profit from their cheap labor; banks were filled with idle reserves and borrowing ceased, although interest rates were below one percent per year; agricultural produces rotted in the fields while people went hungry. More interesting is the fact that even the divorce rate declined, as well as those for marriages and live birth rates per 1,000 of population (Hughes and Cain 1994:444-445). All this led former President Calvin Coolidge to comment with his customary wisdom by the end of 1930 that "When more and more people are thrown out of work, unemployment results." Again in early 1931, Coolidge stated that "This country is not in good condition" (Zinn 1999:387).

By 1931, the percentage of unemployed had reached15.9 percent of the labor force; the gross national product (GNP) was $75.8 billion in current prices or $136.4 per 1958 prices; the Federal receipts totaled $3.2 billion, the expenditure totaled $4.1 billion—i.e. a deficit of $1.1 billion (Hughes and Cain 1994:446). Even more dramatic was the banking industry, which had been a major growth sector, suffered a tremendous blow during the economic crisis. Between 1900 and 1914, the number of commercial banks had reached 31,076. However, between 1921 and 1934, the number of these banks had fallen by 16,305, of which 14,820 were right out failures. In 1929, 659 banks were shut down; in 1930, the doors of 1,352 were shut; and by 1931, 2,294 had been shut (Hughes and Cain 1994:450).

The human toll from the economic crisis was quite acute. Four New York City hospitals alone reported 95 deaths from hunger in 1931. Rampant malnutrition posed the greater threat, as one out of five school children did not get enough to eat. The rural areas were most severely devastated. Southern landless tenant farmers and sharecroppers, most of them African Americans, saw their human spirits crushed by the poverty. In 1930, one-quarter of the total southern population—i.e. eight and half million people, of whom three million were African Americans—lived in tenant and sharecropping families. Most of them were illiterate and penniless, and they crowded into two- and three-room cabins that had no screens or even doors, much less electricity, plumbing, running water, or sanitary wells. Their daily meals were comprised of salt pork, cornmeal, molasses, beans, peas, and whatever they could fish or hunt. They were marred by diseases of dietary and vitamin deficiencies. Economist John Maynard Keynes equated the era of the Great Depression to that of the Dark Ages that lasted four hundred years (Roark et al. 2000:635-636).

The nation was not prepared to meet the human catastrophe, as it had the worst welfare system in the Western world. No federal assistance existed. What assistance framework existed was made up of a small number of voluntary organizations and pinch-penny state and local agencies that offered very little aid. For example, in Philadelphia, the best the city could offer to a family of four without an income was $5.50 per week. Although comparatively generous, it was not enough to live on. In New York City, which had the largest number of welfare cases, only $2.39 was provided per week. And in Detroit, which was devastated when the bottom fell out of the automobile industry, only 60 cents was allotted for a week before the city ran out of money completely (Roark et al. 2000:636).

As the crisis deepened, may Americans looked for scapegoats. Mexican Americans became one of the groups that were thoroughly scapegoated. During the relatively more prosperous era of the 1920s, large farmers brought many Mexican agricultural workers into the country legally. In the 1930s, Mexican Americans were ostracized and characterized as dangerous aliens who took jobs from Americans. Government officials, especially those in Los Angeles County, supported by the Department of Labor, targeted all Mexican residents for deportation, no matter their citizenship status. Consequently, about half a million Mexicans and Mexican Americans were deported or fled to Mexico. Among these were children born in the United States—American citizens who had never lived outside of the country (Roark et al. 2000:636).

Families experienced a great deal of stress, as women left the home to replace their husbands as breadwinners. After many years of rising consumption, the significant decrease in incomes precipitated belt tightening measures. As men fell prey to guilt and loss of self-esteem, women became increasingly assertive and self-reliant. Nonetheless, the divorce rate, as stated earlier, declined, even though family violence, alcoholism, and suicide rate skyrocketed. Since the desperately poor could not afford the legal expense of divorce proceedings, they opted to deserting their families in droves (Roark et al. 2000:636).

President Herbert Hoover's reputation declined as precipitously as the economy declined. As James Roark and his partners recounted,

> Makeshift shantytowns that sprang up on the edges of American cities were called "Hoovervilles." Newspapers used as cover by those sleeping on the streets were "Hoover blankets." An empty pocket turned inside out was a "Hoover flag," and jackrabbits caught for food were "Hoover hogs." Innumerable bitter jokes circulated about Hoover. One gibe asserted that Hoover was the world's greatest engineer: "In a little more than two years he has drained, ditched, and damned the United States." Another story told of Hoover's request of Andrew Mellon for a nickel to call up a friend.

"Here's a dime," Mellon is said ro have replied, "call up all
your friends" (Raork et al. 2000:636).

Hoover's attempt to present a positive spin on the crisis made matters worse. He favored formal dress and manners in the White House
and for dinner, with or without guests, attended by a retinue of valets
and waiters, as a way to express confidence in prosperity. From within
that display of prosperity, Hoover calmly assured Americans that no
one went to bed hungry at night (Roark et al. 2000:636). Obviously, as
Howard Zinn observed, Hoover, like the others who were responsible
for organizing the economy did not know what had happened, were
baffled by it, refused to recognize it, and found reasons other than the
system's failure. Not long before the crash, Hoover had boasted: "We in
America today are nearer to the final triumph over poverty than ever
before in the history of any land" (Zinn 1999:387).

Hoover's administration did not consider it the prerogative of the
federal government to investigate assertions of its sentiment toward the
plight of the society. Walter Gifford, president of the American
Telephone and Telegraph (AT&T) Company whom Hoover appointed
to coordinate private relief efforts, admitted to members of a Senate
subcommittee that he had made no efforts to compile data on the number of people who had lost their jobs and were receiving relief. An exas-
perated Senator Robert La Follette asked if Gifford had any impulse to
know the facts. Gifford's reply underscored the tendency of the nation's
wealthy to distance themselves from the problems that beseeched the
poor. "Well," Gifford is noted to have said genially, "I will not say that I
did not make any estimate for my own interest and amusement" (Roark
et al. 2000:636-637).

Another example of how the nation's wealthy were oblivious toward
the downtrodden is that of automobile magnate Henry Ford. As Zinn
pointed out, Ford, in March 1931, said that the crisis was here because
"the average man won't really do a day's work unless he is caught and

cannot get out of it. There is plenty of work to do if people would do it." A few weeks later, Ford laid off 75,000 of his workers (Zinn 1999:387).

While the wealthy were in a state of denial, other Americans turned to the movies as a means to escape their predicament. It is estimated that between 60 and 75 million people (about 70 percent of the nation's population) managed to scrounge up enough dimes to fill the movie theaters each week. Films that blended the nostalgia for the lost Golden Twenties with the hope that renewed prosperity was around the corner were instant hits. Leading musicals such as *Forty-Second Street* and *Gold Diggers* provided rags-to-riches stories. As conditions continued to deteriorate, film producers turned to grittier stories. Films such as King Vidor's *Our Daily Bread* and John Ford's *The Grapes of Wrath* expressed compassion for the destitute. Gangster films sought to show grim lessons about ill-gotten gains. This was a reflection of the new production code of 1930 that was geared toward protecting public morals. *Public Enemy*, the classic cautionary tale about the doom that will befall a criminal, found a particularly morbid way of rendering the message, as it ended with gangsters delivering the bullet-riddled body of a hoodlum to the doorstep of his saintly, long suffering mother (Roark et al. 2000:637-638).

Hollywood's laudable efforts to keep Americans on the right side of the law did not bear much fruit, as crime increased in the early 30s. People who had lost their farms to bank foreclosures perceived bank robbers as people who were simply taking back from banks what they (i.e. the banks) had stolen from the poor. In his "The Ballad of Pretty Boy Floyd," Woody Gutherie, the populist folk singer from Oklahoma, captured the public's tolerance for outlaws in his widely admired tribute to a murderous bank robber with a choirboy face:

Yes, as through this world I ramble,
I see lots of funny men,
Some will rob you with a six-gun,

Some will rob you with a pen.
But as through your life you'll travel,
Wherever you may roam,
You won't never see an outlaw drive
A family from their home (Roark et al. 2000:638).

The era of the Great Depression also saw an increase in working-class militancy, albeit slowly. Even though the working-class was paying the heaviest price for the crisis, the labor movement, including the dominant American Federation of Labor (AFL), responded in a snail's pace. This was a direct result of the hobbling labor unions encountered during the 1920s from court injunctions that curtailed the rights of unions to organize and strike. During the early stage of the depression, AFL head William Green echoed Hoover's sentiment that the dole will turn the worker into "a ward of the state." However, by 1931, the continuing economic malaise had turned Green into a militant. During the AFL's annual convention that year, Green shouted: "I warn the people who are exploiting the workers that they can drive them only so far before they will turn on them and destroy them. They are taking no account of the history of nations in which governments have been overturned. Revolutions grow out of the depths of hunger" (Roark et al. 2000:638).

Like the labor leaders, it took some time for the American people to become angry. But once they did, they manifested their frustration with strong protest. On the morning of March 7, 1932, several thousand laid off workers arrived at the gates of Ford's River Rouge factory in Dearborn, Michigan to demand that they be rehired. Henry Ford sent out his private security forces to disperse the demonstrators. As the protesters refused and started hurling rocks, the Ford army responded with tear gas and freezing water and quickly escalated to gunfire. By the time the ruckus ended, four demonstrators lay dead and dozens had been wounded. A 40,000 strong outraged public turned out for the unemployed men's funeral. Ford's callous and brutal resort to violence was denounced in editorials and at protest rallies throughout the nation (Roark et al. 2000:638).

Soon afterward, farmers, desperately needing relief, mounted their own uprising. When the United States Congress rejected the farmers' demand to guarantee farm prices that would at least equal the cost of production, about 3,000 farmers, spearheaded by the flamboyant Milo Reno, formed the National Farmers' Holiday Association (NFHA) to force farmers to take a "holiday" from delivering produce to the market. Reno and his followers, invoking the Boston Tea Party of December 1773, barricaded roads around Sioux City, Iowa, turned back farmers going to market, and dumped thousands of gallons of milk in ditches. The rebellion raised general awareness of farm grievances, even though it was short-lived and did not force a critical shortage of food. With what they referred to as "penny sales," militant farmers had fuller material effect. When farmers defaulted on their mortgages and their farms were put up for auction, their neighbors would pack the auctions and, after warning others not to bid, would then buy the foreclosed properties for a few pennies and return them to the bankrupt owners. This strategy forced some states to suspend farmers' debts or reduce their mortgages (Roark et al. 2000:638).

In the very large agricultural holdings of California, farms and labor leaders joined their forces. More than 50,000 farm workers, most of them Mexicans, went on strike when landowners cut their already meager wages to laborers in what one critic dubbed as "factories in the fields." John Simpson, president of the National Farmers Union (NFU), reflecting the strife mounting throughout the nation, affirmed that "the biggest and finest crop of revolutions you ever saw is sprouting all over the country right now" (Roark et al. 2000:638).

The economic crisis also led to the revival of the left in the United States. The death of Eugene Debs had also led to the demise of the Socialist Party. The Great Depression, a signal of the great failure of Western capitalism, gave back life to the socialist movement and the

American Communist Party grew to its greatest size and influence in American history. Believing that only an overthrow of the capitalist system could save the victims of the depression, about 100,000 disillusioned American workers, intellectuals and college students joined the Communist Party. Having increased the size of the National Miners Union (NMU) from 100 to 25,000, the party, in 1931, went to Harlan County, Kentucky to show its solidarity with strikers of harshly oppressed coal miners. The violence unleashed by the mine owners' thugs against the strikers was riveted by newspapers and newsreels throughout the country. Although the miners were beaten down, the Communist Party did gain the reputation as the most dedicated and fearless champion of the plight of working people (Roark et al. 2000:638-639).

As racism also increased, the left was equally ready to challenge that vestige of American society. While the major parties—the Democratic and Republican—were reluctant to challenge the system of segregation in the South, the Socialist Party, led by moral reformer Norman Thomas, championed the fight to dismantle the sharecropping system that left many African Americans in poverty and virtual servitude. When nine young African American men (who later came to be called the Scottsboro Nine) were arrested on trumped-up rape charges, a team of lawyers was sent by the Communist Party to defend them. These seasoned lawyers were able to save the young men from the electric chair. The party also challenged efforts by Alabama plantation owners to evict their African American tenants. While the Communist party was unable to force much change on the deeply entrenched southern ideology, it was able to briefly attract new converts. The number of African Americans who joined the party rose from only about 30 members in 1930 to about 10,000 by the end of the 30s before most of the converts returned to traditional reform movements rooted in constitutional rights and religious conviction (Roark et al. 2000:639).

Among the prominent African Americans in the Communist party were Hosea Hudson, the organizer of the unemployed in Birmingham,

Alabama, and Angelo Herndon, whose father died of miner's pneumonia, who had worked in mines as a boy in Kentucky, and joined an Unemployment Council (UC) in Birmingham (Zinn 1999:447). Hudson, who was born in rural Georgia, became a plow-hand at the age of ten, and later became an iron worker in Birmingham, was aroused by the case of the Scottsboro Nine in 1931. That same year, Hudson joined the Communist Party; and in 1932 and 1933, he organized unemployed African Americans in Birmingham (Zinn 1999:398). Herndon became a Communist Party organizer in Atlanta. In 1932, he and his comrades organized block committees of UCs which won rent relief for the needy. They also organized a demonstration that attracted 1,000 people, of which 600 were white, and the next day the city voted $6,000 in relief to the jobless. Soon after that, however, Herndon was arrested, held incommunicado, and charged with violating a Georgia anti-insurrection statute. Herndon was convicted and spent five years in jail until the Supreme Court in 1937 ruled unconstitutional the Georgia statute under which he was found guilty (Zinn 1999:447-448).

Indeed, the year 1931 witnessed the height of action by the left and protests by workers and farmers who bore the brunt of the Great Depression. Breadlines, soup kitchens, foreclosures, unemployment, and despair precipitated patriotic Americans to question the ethos of capitalism. As a Wisconsin farmer is cited to have explained, "I am as conservative as any man could be, but any economic system that has in its power to set me and my wife in the streets, at my age—what can I see but red?" (Roark et al. 2000:639).

American University, like the rest of the country, was severely hit by the Great Depression of the 1930s. By 1931, the University's student population had dwindled dramatically because many people could not afford tuition. It was through the generous support of the Methodist Church that the University's administrators managed to keep the institution open (wysiwyg://134/http:www.american.edu/tour/history.html).   Thus,   the optimistic tone of the University's Alma Mater and School Song must have been inspired by a somewhat melancholy strain: Most Americans, including those at American University, were far from being optimistic at the height of the Great Depression.

Other American University School Songs

The American University Library Archives, thanks to the diligent work of George Arnold (University Archivist) and Ignacio Moreno (Assistant University Archivist), has catalogued the earliest and later known copies of the University's Alma Maters and Fight Songs. The first of these songs is the following that was featured in the 1929 *Aucola* and titled "American Alma Mater." The words of the song were written by Pauline A. Frederick (Class of 1930), the music was arranged by R. Deane Shurr, and it was copyrighted by the American University Glee Club. This song also appeared in the 1930-1931 and the 1931-1932 editions of the *American University Student Handbook* with the title "College Song."

American Alma Mater

Firm on a sweep of campus
　Stands the American U.,
Builded with vision and labor,
　Pioneer dream come true;
Namesake of our great nation,
　Nurtured in ideals high.
American–Alma Mater,
　Behold–they banners fly!
American–Alma Mater,
　Lead on–the day is new;
The march begun must yet be won
　To the glory of Orange and Blue.

II

Orange from a new day's sunrise
　Caught in the folds of Blue,
Holding in deathless ensign
　A glory that is A. U.,
Symbol of A. U.'s dawning
　In life that is greater to be,
American–Alma Mater,
　The shrine of our loyalty.

American–Alma Mater,
　Laid on, etc.

The following song appeared in the 1931-1932 edition of the *American University Student Handbook* as "Days that We Treasure," in the 1933-1934 edition of the *Student Activities of the College of Liberal Arts of American University* handbook as "Alma Mater," and also in the 1945-1946 edition of the *American University College of Arts and Sciences Freshman Bible* edited by Ann Graham as "Alma Mater."

Alma Mater

All students stand when this is played

Tomorrows pass so soon behind us
Into shadows of the past–
So the years will often find us.
Calling days that flew so fast.

Refrain

Come, come, days that we treasure,
We live in you–
We yearn now for the pleasure
At college we knew;
Friendships will always bind us;
In youth we live, for mem'ries remind us
Of Orange and Blue–
Come, days fullest in measure
Of our A.U.

The following Sports Fight Song titled "We've Got A Team" appeared in the 1930-1931 and 1931-1932 editions of the *American University Student Handbook*. The words of the song were written by John Houston, and the music was arranged by Clair Altland.

We've Got A Team

Without exaggeration
  We've got a combination,
An A-1 aggregation
  Of all-star (Basketeers).
              (Pigskin Men).
You see our weather vane shows
  Our every sky has rainbows,
And everyone that's sane knows
  Our team (need have no fears).
              (will win again).

Refrain

We've got a team! (Rah! Rah! Rah!)
  We've got a victory
  We're gonna hang up as our score–
We've got the fight! (Yea, team, fight!)
  We want the world to see.
   We've got the fight and something more–
Hear that shout! Hear that yell!
  Without a doubt we'll give them–
  What they asked for!
We've got a team! (Rah! Rah! Rah!)
  We've got a victory
  We're gonna hang up our score!

The following song entitled "A.U. Pledge Song" appeared in the 1931-1932 edition of the *American University Student Handbook*. The words were written by Anne King and the music was composed by Louise Murray.

A.U. Pledge Song

Till the height of the campus be leveled
  In the dust of an ageless day;
Till the echoes that live in the halls we love
  Like the mist dimly pass away;
Till the blue and the orange shall blend,
  And the wings of the eagle shall fail,
We will stand, true of heart for American–
  Hail, our Alma mater, Hail!

In the 1947 and 1948 editions of the *American University Freshman Yearbook*, nothing called Alma Mater appeared. What appeared was the following "College Hymn."

College Hymn

Ancient fort of our high campus
This our school.
A steady compass
Help us now stand firm
Pointing to the light
In a world of doubt and conflict
Seeks the lodestar of the spirit
Help us now stand firm
Pointing to the light
May the years we spend at college
Symbol of true loyalty
Build a bastion brave with knowledge
May the compass ever be
Help us stand firm
Point to the light
Help us stand firm
Point to the light

The 1947 and 1948 editions of the *American University Freshman* also had the following Sports Fight Song.

Sports Fight Song

Fight that team across the field
Oh, Orange and Blue (*repeat*)
Eagle banners never yield

American U., American U.

Set the earth reverberating
With the glory old and new.
Fight on triumphantly,
And proudly bring the victory to old A.U.

Come, now comrades true,
Sing for old A.U.
We're all pals together
Eagles of one feather
So let us raise our voices high
In the triumph cry.
Aims, ambitions, in the sky and victory ours.

Loyal Eagles, hit them hard, and
See how they fall (*repeat*)
Fighting Eagles, never let that
Team get the ball (*repeat*).

Set the earth reverberating
With all the glory old and new.
Fight on triumphantly
And proudly bring the victory to old A.U.

Finally, the following song entitled "Dear Old A.U." appeared in the 1949 edition of the *American University Freshman Notes*. The words and music of the song were composed by Michael L. Moore (Class of 1949) and copyrighted in 1948.

Dear Old A.U.

Dear old A.U. we toast to thee,
Pledge our honor, our loyalty.
We'll remember Red White and Blue,
The pride and glory that we knew.
Noble college of days serene,
Golden friendships, familiar scenes.
Bonds will hold us forever true
To Alma Mater Old A.U. Dear U.

A common feature in all of the songs, no matter in which epoch they were written, is their manifestation of optimism. Thus, the songs can be seen not only as sociocultural texts, but also as important vehicles for understanding the psyche of the American University student—her/his individual and group identity; her/his emotional and intellectual point of view. The composers of the songs saw American University as a place where learning defines duties and responsibilities alongside obligations and rights. All these aspects relate to the various activities that have to do with the survival of American University. The survival concept is continuing, dynamic, and dialectical. The fundamental principle that is at the basis of this concept is a moral one.

Endnotes

1. *Context-shaped* means that a speaker's communicative action is a "contribution to an on-going sequence of actions [that] cannot adequately be understood except by reference to the context–including, especially, the immediately preceding configuration of actions–in which it participates" (Heritage 1984:242).

2. *Context-renewing* refers to "the character of conversational actions [that] is directly related to the fact that they are context shaped...the context of a next action is repeatedly renewed with every current action" (Heritage 1984:242).

3. But even more primary, it is the role that context helps to create.

Chapter 4

Deixis

In this chapter, the deixis embedded in the texts of the American University Alma Mater and Fight Song are discussed. The word *deixis*, as Lyons pointed out, comes from a Greek word meaning "pointing" or "indicating" and "is now employed in linguistics to refer to the function of personal and demonstrative pronouns, of tense and of a variety of other grammatical and lexical features which relate utterances to the spatio-temporal co-ordinates of the act of utterance" (1977:636). Thus, as Levinson later observed, the single most obvious way in which the relationship between language and context is reflected in the structures of languages is through deixis. Essentially, according to Levinson, deixis deals with the ways in which languages encode or grammaticalize features of the *context of utterance* or *speech event*, and therefore also deals with ways in which the interpretation of utterances hinges upon the analysis of that context of utterance (1983:54). As Hoffman later stated, deictic or pointing words exist in all languages and are very useful for "referring" to objects around us (1993:61).

Combining traditional (1-3 below) and contemporary categorizations (4 and 5 below) of deixis, Levinson has developed the following five categories within which they can be subsumed (1993:62-63):

(1) *Person deixis* encode the *role* of participants in a speech event in which the utterance in question is delivered—i.e. *first person* encodes

the speaker's reference to her/himself, *second person* encodes the speaker's reference to one or more addresses, and *third person* encodes the reference of persons and entities which are neither speakers nor addresses of the utterance in question.

(2) *Place or Space deixis* encodes spatial location *relative* to the location of the participants in the speech events—i.e. *proximal* encodes closeness to speaker, and *distal* encodes non-proximal or sometimes closeness to the addressee.

(3) *Time deixis* encodes temporal points and spans *relative* to the time at which an utterance was spoken, or a written message inscribed—this time is referred to as *coding time* or CT, which is distinct from *receiving time* or RT.

(4) *Discourse or Text deixis* encodes reference to portions of the unfolding discourse in which the utterance, which includes the text referring expression, is located.

(5) *Social deixis* encodes social distinctions that are relative to participants-roles, particularly aspects of the social relationship holding between speaker and addressee(s) or speaker and some referent.

System in Deixis

According to Hofmann (1993:70), every language possesses a systematic arrangement of deictic words, demonstrating that those words have meanings that can be divided into smaller pieces that can be referred to as "semantic *atoms*," as long as they do not need further divisions. He added that while, for example, English, Spanish and Japanese are different at a superficial level, hence a reason we seldom translate them word for word, nevertheless, a closer look at the semantic elements underlying these languages' systems reveals amazing similarities. Hofmann cited the fact that English can express the same distances as Japanese deictic elements by combining the [Spk = close to the speaker] contrast between *here, there* with the [Awa = not close to either speaker or addressee] contrast in *to come, to go.*

Also, Hofmann (1993:71) noted that a word's **collocation,** i.e. what it can be combined with semantically, can yield strong indications of its meaning. Solely, however, these collocations are not proof and should be accepted with a grain of salt.

Hofmann (1973:71) further pointed out that the similarities in semantic elements indicate the notion that humans might all possess the same ones from which words are developed. Thus, he suggested that it is not farfetched to suspect that we humans have the same building blocks of articulate thought because of our nature. However, he also noted that this concept of universally shared elements is not evident in words, as languages differ widely even in their central aspects such as deixis for what words they have and their meanings.

Deictic Context

Brown and Yule suggested the notion of *deictic context* as a way of imposing some sort of analytic structure on what they referred to as the "lumpen mass of context." They defined *deictic context* as "those features which will permit interpretation for deictic expressions like the temporal expression *now*, the spatial expression *here*, and the first person expression *I*" (1983:50).

In probing the question whether or not standard procedures exist for determining what information is relevant to the interpretation of deictic expressions, Brown and Yule referred to the following suggestion by Lyons that, in principle, there might be such standard procedures:

Every actual utterance is spatiotemporally unique, being spoken or written at a particular place and at a particular time;
and provided that there is some standard system for identifying points in space and time, we can, in principle, specify the
actual spatiotemporal situation of any utterance act [by giving its spatiotemporal co-ordinates with the framework of
the standard system (Brown and Yule 1983:51, cited from
Lyons 1977:570).

Following Lyons' reasoning, Brown and Yule, therefore, asserted that
standard systems clearly exist for locating points in time and space.
They also suggested that the further away in time the message was situated, the less likely the speaker will recall the precise date and time at
which it took place, and the larger the time-span s/he is likely to state
that it occurred. Thus, Brown and Yule reasoned that it is unlikely, then,
that standard procedures of recoding space and time will be relevant to
the unique identification of utterance acts (1983:51).

Brown and Yule (1983:55) further suggested that the deictic center is
located within the context of utterance by the speaker, but that interpreting the expression *now* as relating duratively or subsequently to the
utterance, and the time-span involved, ought to be determined in terms
of the utterance's content. They also noted that the fixing of the deictic
center is particularly germane to what Lyons (1977:637) referred to as

the canonical situation of utterance: this involves one-one, or
one-many, signaling in the phonic medium along the vocal-
auditory channel, with all the participants present in the same
actual situation able to see one another and to perceive the
associated non-vocal paralinguistic features of their utterances, and each assuming the role of sender and receiver in
turn (quoted in Brown and Yule 1983:53).

Thus, for Brown and yule, it is, of course, possible to employ the expressions *here* and *now* in what they referred to as "misplaced contexts" (1983:53).

Brown and Yule also cautioned that space-time co-ordinates should be regarded as simple unconstructed cues for interpreting context. Similarly, they urged that the other co-ordinates relevant to deictic context—*speaker, hearer* and *indicated object*—must not be perceived as simple unconstructed cues which demand standard specification (1983:53-54).

Demonstratives and the Definite Article

As Lyons suggested, demonstrative pronouns and adjectives, such as 'this' and 'that' in English, and demonstrative adverbs, such as 'here' and 'there,' are fundamentally deictic. Functioning in this capacity, he added, they should be interpreted based on the location of the participants in the deictic context. The distinction between 'this' and 'that,' Lyons posited, hinges upon the proximity to the zero-point of the deictic context (1977:646).

From a diachronic perspective, according to Lyons, the definite article in English ('the') is a demonstrative adjective that is not inflected for gender and number; the third-person personal pronouns ('she,' 'he,' and 'it') are demonstrative pronouns, distinguished in terms of gender and number. However, like the definite article, the third-person personal pronouns are unmarked for proximity (1977:647).

Lyons pointed out that in many languages, distinctions of proximity are lexicalized or grammaticalized in the proximal systems. This is also the case for gender, number and status. He added that other languages lexicalized or grammaticalized distinctions of gender that are based on size, shape, function, texture, etc., not on sex. Also, spatial distinctions in these other languages hinge upon visibility, the speaker's normal habits, the points of the compass, some salient landmarks, and so on.

The function of the demonstrative pronoun, according to Lyons, is to get the addressee to pay attention implied by the use of the pronoun in terms of gender, number, status, etc. (1977:647-648).

Lyons further suggested two ways an object can be identified by means of referring expressions. The first way involves informing the addressee where the object is (i.e. by locating it for her/him). The second way is by telling her/him what the object is like, what properties it possesses or to what class of objects it belongs (i.e. by describing it for her/him). Either or both kinds of information, according to Lyons, can be encoded in the demonstrative and personal pronouns of certain language-systems. The more information, whether locative or qualitative, that is encoded in the deictic expression, asserted Lyons, the easier the addressee can identify its referent (1977:648).

The deictic, observed Lyons, could refer to either an entity or a place. This ambivalence leads to a subsequent syntactic distinction between employing it as a pronoun and employing it as an adverb. It always functions as an adverbial in a predicative expression (1977:450).

In English, two adverbial deictics can be distinguished in terms of proximity: 'there' : 'here.' Also, two adverbial deictics can be distinguished in terms of proximity: 'this' : 'that,' with the forms *this, these* : *that, those.* Thus 'this' and 'here' are proximal while 'that' and 'there' are non-proximal. The situation for pronominal deictics is more complex, as the third-person singular pronouns (i.e. 'she,' 'he,' 'it'), on the one hand, are distinguished for gender, but not for proximity. However, the demonstrative pronouns, on the other hand, are distinguished for proximity and number, but not for gender, and their forms are similar to those of the demonstrative adjectives. To make matters even more complex is the fact that the definite article behaves syntactically like the demonstrative adjectives, but it is neutral in terms of proximity, gender, and number. Moreover, the definite article derives, historically, from the non-proximal demonstrative adjective 'that' (Lyons 1977:650).

With this backdrop, Lyons went on to extend the system by introduc-
ing a distinction of gender based on sex. In doing so, he assumed that
'this' and 'that' must not be utilized pronominally to refer to persons
(except in constructions in which they can be used in ordinary English)
and that 'she' or 'he' should be used instead. He also assumed that 'it' has
replaced 'that' in its deictically neutral sense. He then suggested that, in
terms of this analysis of the meaning and syntactic function of the
third-person pronouns—'she,' 'he,' and 'it'—are all variants of the deictically neutral pronominal 'that.' And, thus, these third-person pronouns differ in that 'she' encapsulates the meaning of 'female,' 'he'
encapsulates the meaning of 'male,' and 'it' is a syntactically determined
variant of 'that' which does not encapsulate either 'female' or male' but
something like 'non-personal.' Lyons added that encapsulation can be
formalized in terms of universal sense-components (1977:651-652).

Deixis, Anaphora and Cataphora

As Lyons (1977:659) pointed out, pronouns are traditionally conceived of having two distinct, albeit related, functions: (1) deixis and (2)
anaphora[1]*/cataphora.*[2] Their anaphoric/cataphoric function can be
illustrated by means of the statements like the following:

Ali ate lunch early and he was full

in which 'he' refers to the antecedent—i.e. the expression 'Ali,' and
'Ali' refers to the antecedent that precedes the anaphoric pronoun 'he.'
What underlies the notion of anaphoric (and, of course, cataphoric)
reference, according to Lyons, is the principle of substitution in the
Bloomfieldian sense—i.e. a grammatical process or relationship. This,
Lyons maintained, is the historical source for what became the standard
treatment of pronouns in Chomskyan generative grammar (Lyons
1977:659).

As Lyons further noted, anticipatory anaphora (or cataphora) does not hold between co-ordinate clauses in compound sentences—a restriction that is common in a number of languages. He hypothesized that this may be because a complex sentence is a grammatically more cohesive unit than a compound sentence. However that may be, he also argued, anticipatory anaphora (or cataphora) is far from being as free as the anaphora (1977:661).

Thus, Lyons asserted that whether a pronoun is interpreted as having anaphoric/cataphoric or deictic reference (or both) would seem to hinge primarily upon the context-of-utterance and cannot be decided within a microlinguistic analysis of the structure and meaning of the sentence. He also noted that the emphatic or contrastive function of heavy stress is independent of its deictic function, and that the one includes the other (1977:661-662).

Deixis in the Songs

The following deixis were delineated after examining the texts of the American University Alma Mater and Fight Song:

Deixis Type	Alma Mater	Fight Song
1. Person	(a) our	(a) the mighty AU Eagles
	(b) us	(b) we
	(c) we	(c) you
	(d) you	(d) enemy
2. Time	(a) college years	(a) when
	(b) the past	
	(c) years	
	(d) days	
	(e) now	

3. Place or
   Space   (a) college   (a) AU
                  (b) AU

Person, time and place or space deixis exist in the American University Alma Mater and Fight Song. Discourse or text and social deixis are absent.

All four person deixis in the Alma Mater are second-person pronouns; two of the person deixis in the Fight Song are second- person pronouns, and the other two indicate American University athletes (called the "AU Eagles") and their opponents (referred to as the "enemy"). The five time deixis in the Alma Mater indicate the past, the present, and the future, and the single time deixis in the Fight Song indicates the future. The two place or space deixis in the Alma Mater and the one in the Fight Song all indicate American University.

Indeed, in order to interpret the preceding deictic forms, contextual knowledge was required. Thus, deixis is not reducible to matters of truth-conditional semantics.

Endnotes

1. *Anaphora* is a pronoun that follows the expression with which it is correlated.

2. *Cataphora* is a pronoun that precedes the expression with which it is correlated.

Chapter 5

Presuppositions

The rhetorical tactic of presupposition in academic discourse is by now familiar to many linguists. A paradigm example is the professor's query, "Did that student fail his mathematics course again?" Without explicitly making the assertion, the professor implies that the student has indeed failed his mathematics course before based on the iterative 'again.' A less contentious presupposition can be suggested as well: that the student is a male in light of the pronoun 'his.' This example illustrates the fact that speakers or writers often express more than they assert. Their utterances or scripts convey not only their surface contents, but a great deal of auxiliary content as well.

In this chapter, the linguistic presuppositions in the texts of the American University Alma Mater and Fight Song are identified and analyzed. The concept presupposition is first defined and its scope clearly delimited. This is done by briefly examining it as it has developed in the philosophical and linguistic literature.[1]

Logical Presupposition

The phenomenon of linguistic presupposition can be traced back to the philosophical writings of Gottlob Frege (1892/1952). He raised many of the issues that later became central to the discussion of presupposition.

According to Frege, "If anything is asserted there is always an obvious presupposition (*voraussetzung*) that the simple or compound proper names used have a reference" (1952:69).

A later exchange between Bertrand Russell (1905, 1957) and Peter Strawson (1950, 1952) brought the notion of presupposition more fully into scholarly discourse. Russell, in his first essay on the subject (1905), argued that Frege's views were simply wrong. Struggling with the problem of how to account for the fact that sentences lacked proper referents, Russell came up with conclusions that were different from those of Frege.

Russell's analysis remained unchallenged until Strawson, in his 1950 essay, suggested a different approach. For Strawson, many of the puzzles in Russell's essay emerged from a failure to distinguish sentences from uses of sentences to make, for instance, statements that are true or false. Consider the following sentences.

(1) The King of Great Britain is a tyrant.

(2) The King of Great Britain is not a tyrant.

(3) There is one and only one King of Great Britain.

In his analysis of definite descriptions, Russell suggested that propositions of the form (1) entail presuppositions of the form (3). Strawson did not agree with this suggestion. Instead, Strawson pointed out that (2), the negation of (1), does not affect the truth conditions of (3). If the relation between (1) and (3) were one of entailment, then, by *modus ponens*[2] (2) could not entail (3). One's linguistic intuitions tell her/him, however, that if *either* (1) or (2) is true, then, (3) is also true. Strawson labeled the relation one of presupposition, which he formally designated as:

(4) Sentence S_1 logically presupposes sentence S_2 iff the truth of S_2 is a precondition for the truth or falsity of S_1 (1952:175).

The practical approach for distinguishing presuppositions from entailments is the employment of the traditional *constancy under negation* rule. One sentence is said to presuppose another if and only if the sentence and its negation both require it to be true.

Semantic Presupposition and Implications for Logic

Intrigued by Strawson's account of presupposition, formal linguists sought to build semantic theory upon the foundational relation of semantic entailment defined in (5), and had hoped to advance a more convincingly logical account of natural language by suggesting the relation of semantic presupposition defined in (6), as follows:

(5) S_1 semantically entails S_2 (written S_1, $\Vdash$S), iff every situation that makes S_1 true makes S_2 true.

(6) A sentence S_1 semantically presupposes a sentence S_2 iff S_1 $\Vdash$S and $\sim S_1$ $\Vdash S_2$.

In order to incorporate the relation of semantic presupposition into a formal natural-language semantics, a logical framework that is different from the standard calculi is called for. This means that *bivalence*[3] and *modus tollens*[4] must be given up in order to meet the requirement for semantic presupposition. If a sentence S_1 semantically presupposes a sentence S_2, then, by definition (6), S_1 entails S_2 and $\sim S_1$ entails S_2. *Modus tollens* must, thus, be given up. For without *bivalency*, in propositions of the form p→q, the falsity of the consequent could not falsify the condition. The consequent might instead result in the truth value 'neither true nor false.'

Presuppositional Defeasibility

Presuppositional defeasibility refers to the fact that presuppositions are liable to evaporate in certain contexts, either immediate linguistic contexts, less immediate discourse contexts, or in cases where contrary assumptions are made. The defeasibility of presuppositions in particular discourse contexts, for example, can defeat any context-free semantic account as illustrated in the following sentences:

(7) School of International Service alumna Petra Kelly was elected to the German Bundestag before she could realize her dream of equal rights and justice for everyone in Germany.

(8) School of International Service alumna Petra Kelly realized her dream of equal rights and justice for everyone in Germany.

(9) School of International Service alumna Petra Kelly was assassinated before she could realize her dream of equal rights and justice for everyone in Germany.

The connectives 'before' and 'after' ordinarily trigger the presuppositions of their complements, as (7) presupposes (8). But in (9), the meaning of 'before' (temporal priority) plus background knowledge about assassination defeat the presupposition of (8). Individuals ordinarily do not realize their dreams after their assassination.

In this situation, temporal logic will not help. Presuppositions are defeasible within many constructions such as those in the following sentences.

(10) If George Bush selects David Duke as his running mate, Bush will regret having a racist on his ticket.

(11) If George Bush selects Collin Powell as his running mate, Bush will regret having a racist on his ticket.

(12) George Bush will have a racist on his ticket.

The sentence (11) presupposes (12), but (10) does not. Since the selection of David Duke, well known for his racist pronouncements, would prove to be an action Bush would regret, the conditional clause in (10) defeats the presupposition of (12). The fact that Collin Powell is not generally thought to be a racist, 'racist' in (11) must refer to someone else and the conditional clause does not defeat the presupposition.

Examples such as this would place presupposition outside the domain of context-free logical semantics, but within the scope of a context-sensitive linguistic semantics. The incorporation of propositions drawn from lexical entries, nonetheless, fails to account for all forms of presuppositional defeasibility. The contents of the following discourse, for example, can defeat a presupposition.

(13) We need to find out which heads of state are on the payroll of the CIA. Bush would certainly know. Bush is not aware that President X is on the payroll of the CIA. So Bush can be trusted.

The sentence 'Bush is not aware that President X is on the payroll of the CIA' would ordinarily presuppose that 'President X is on the payroll of the CIA.' But the preceding discourse defeats this presupposition. It appears that any semantics of presupposition, then, calls for access to the discourse context in order to detect defeated presuppositions. As in the case of lexical access, the mechanisms needed to account for presuppositions gravitate away from semantics and toward pragmatics in this case as well.

Iterative presuppositional defeat causes more havoc. Consider this example:

(14) It is not Thomas Jefferson who will become our first President.

(15) Someone will become our first President.

Ordinarily, sentence (14) will presuppose sentence (15). Suppose, however, that each attendant of the Philadelphia Constitutional Convention of 1787 had asked the utterer of (14), 'Will I be the first President?' to which the response is 'No.' By iterating over the set of attendants at the Convention and proposing that each, in turn, will not be the first President, the presupposition in (15) is defeated. Appeals to lexical knowledge will definitely fail to explain the defeat of the presupposition in this example. Reference to the *deictic context*[5] of the discourse is necessary in order to explain the defeat of the presupposition of (15).

The Projection Problem

There exist two sides to the projection problem. The first is that presuppositions tend to survive in linguistic contexts where entailments cannot. More precisely, the presuppositions of component sentences are inherited by the whole complex sentence where the entailments of those components would not be. The second is that presuppositions tend to disappear in other contexts where one might expect them to survive, and where entailments would.

Beginning with the kind of context in which presuppositions survive where entailments do not, the examples that follow suggest that one may, but need not, take this as a defining characteristic of presuppositions.

(16) President Benjamin Ladner appointed five new administrators.

(17) There is a President.

(18) President Benjamin Ladner appointed three new administrators.

If sentence (16) is negated, as in (19), the entailment (18) does not survive, but the presupposition (17) does; this being, of course, the initial observation from which presuppositional theories emerged.

(19) President Benjamin Ladner did not appoint five new administrators.

In a similar manner, presuppositions survive in other kinds of contexts in which entailments do not. An example is modal contexts: that is, those embedding under modal operators such as *possible, may be, most probably,* etc. Consequently, (20) continues to presuppose (17).

(20) It is possible that President Benjamin Ladner appointed five new administrators.

It is obvious, however, that (20) does not entail (18). One cannot logically infer from the mere possibility of a state of affairs that any part of it is actual.

Presuppositions tend to distinguish themselves by their ability to survive in different sets of contexts like compound sentences formed by connectives *and, or, if...then* and their equivalents. Consider the following examples.

(21) The two Congressman's sons are hired again this term, which entails *inter alia,* (22) and presupposes (23) because of the iterative *again.*

(22) A Congressman's son is hired this term.

(23) The Two Congressman's sons had been hired before.

If (21) is embedded in the antecedent of a conditional like in (24),

(24) If the two Congressman's sons are hired again this term, Senator John Doe will get the support he desperately needs,

it is evident that (22) is not an entailment of (24), but the presupposition (23) survives.

Now turning to the second aspect of the projection problem, in which presuppositions of lower clauses sometimes fail to be inherited by the whole complex sentence, one would observe that presuppositions are sometimes defeasible because of *intra-sentential* context.

Presuppositions can be overtly *denied* in co-ordinate sentences such as:

(25) Benjamin Franklin didn't manage to become President.

(26) Benjamin Franklin tried to become President.

(27) Benjamin Franklin didn't manage to become President; he didn't even run.

Here, (25) presupposes (26), but overt denial defeats it in (27).

In addition, to the overt denial of presuppositions, they can also be suspended in conditional clauses, as for example in:

(28) George Bush didn't lie to the American people again about imposing new taxes.

(29) George Bush previously lied to the American people about imposing new taxes.

(30) George Bush didn't lie to the American people again about imposing new taxes, if indeed he ever did.

In this example, (28) presupposes (29), but the condition in (30) defeats it.

In sum, the above discussion clearly suggests that semantic theories of presupposition are not viable. This is mainly because semantics is more concerned with the specification of invariant, stable meanings that can be associated with expressions.

Pragmatic Presupposition

Because presuppositions are not invariant and they are not stable, they became an ideal unit of linguistic analysis for pragmaticists. Earlier pragmatic theories of presupposition offered little more than possible definitions for the concept using pragmatic notions (Gazdar 1979:103ff has offered a list of these definitions and a discussion). Despite their differing terminology, these definitions have been subsumed by Levinson (1983: 204-205) into two basic concepts: (a) *appropriateness* (or *felicity*), and (b) *mutual knowledge* (or *common ground*, or *joint assumption*) indicated as follows:

(31) An utterance A *pragmatically presupposes* a proposition B iff A is appropriate only if B is *mutually known* by participants.

Levinson, however, argued that the utility of the notion of appropriateness is objectionable and that the mutual knowledge condition is far too strong. He supported Gazdar's (1979:105) suggestion that what one presupposes is *consistent with* the propositions assumed in the context (Levinson 1983:205).

Consequently, an earlier definition of pragmatic presupposition offered by Stalnaker (1974) is still prevalent today. He defined this concept in the following way:

(32) A proposition *P* is a pragmatic presupposition of a speaker just in case the speaker assumes or believes that *P*, assumes or believes that his addressee assumes or believes that *P*, and assumes or believes that his addressee recognized that he is making these assumptions (Stalnaker 1974:200).

Stalnaker's definition suggests that, unless they explicitly object, participants in a discourse implicitly accept the presuppositions of the utterances of other participants. Consequently, the addressee's failure to object to infelicitous presuppositions would violate Grice's maxim of quantity, which calls for a participant's contribution to a discourse be as informative as required for the purpose of communication.

In a later study, Stalnaker (1978) discerned two types of discourse contexts: *defective* and *non-defective*. The former contexts, according to Stalnaker, are inherently unstable and necessarily result in efforts to equilibrate the "context sets" of participants. The latter contexts, Stalnaker suggested, are the "context sets," or the possible worlds that speakers take to be live options, which do not vary from participant to participant.

At a pragmatic level of analysis, then, the defeasibility problem in presupposition can be overcome by employing linguistic procedures that represent textual contents that call for access to the lexical properties of terms, the previously represented contents in the discourse context itself, and the deictic context of utterances. But this still leaves unsolved the projection problem in presupposition.

Fortunately, Gazdar (1979) provided potential analysts with a set of procedures that correctly predict the defeat of presuppositions, even in cases where presuppositional compositionality fails to hold. Gazdar suggested that one identifies all the *possible* presuppositions of a sentence, no matter the defeasibility or projection concerns. Once the actual assertion is represented, one can then enter its entailments, followed by its conversational implicatures. Only then can one employ a canceling mechanism to determine the plausible presuppositions, eliminating those presuppositions that are logically inconsistent with the discourse as represented. Whatever survives is then added to the representation. In essence, an analyst must mark the representations of presuppositions so that they can be retracted if, later in the discourse, they are contradicted by assertional contents.

Gazdar's procedures are framed in terms of the individual speaker. Put differently, the actual presuppositions are those members of the set of possible presuppositions that are consistent with what a speaker has previously asserted, entailed, implicated, and presupposed. Levinson (1983:212n) suggested that Gazdar's procedures can be extended to what discourse participants jointly presume, as called for by Stalnaker's definition of pragmatic presupposition formerly quoted in (32).

Presuppositions in the Songs

The following presuppositions are extracted from the American University Alma Mater:

(33) There exists a past.

(34) Days usually do fly fast.

(35) Days that are treasured and lived in do come.

(36) People yearn.

(37) College can be pleasurable.

(38) Friendships bind and remind people of college colors.

(39) Days fullest in measure of American University do come.

For the American Fight Song, the following presuppositions are identified:

(40) American University Eagles (athletic teams) are mighty.

(41) There have been or will be fights.

(42) American University's colors are red, white and blue.

(43) American University has enemies.

(44) American University is expected or ought to be victorious.

Presuppositions (33), (37) and (40) are triggered by the definite descriptions "the past," "the pleasures of college" and "the might AU Eagles," respectively. As presupposition triggers, definite descriptions, according to Russell (1905, 1957), have nothing like the simple logical translation that we might imagine. Although they occur in actual language as subjects, in logical form they are not logical subjects at all but correspond instead to conjunctions of propositions.

Presuppositions (34), (38), (43) and (44) are triggered by the implicative predicates "recalling days that flew past," "bind us and remind us," "'ll conquer" and "join in and give a yell," respectively. According to Kartunnen (1971:340), implicative predicates carry presuppositions that represent a necessary and sufficient condition for the truth of their complement sentences. An asserted main sentence with an implicative verb commits the writer/speaker to an implied proposition which consists of a complement sentence as augmented by the tense and other modifiers of the main sentence.

Presuppositions (35), (36) and (39) are triggered by the factive verbs "come," "yearn" and "come," respectively. Factive verbs, according to Kiparski and Kiparski (1971:345-346) trigger the presuppositions of their clausal complements.

Finally, presuppositions (41) and 42) are triggered by the temporal clauses "when there is a fight" and "when we wear," respectively. As Frege (1892/1952) suggested, presuppositions triggered by temporal clauses are unaffected by the negation of the main verbs.

Indeed, the preceding presupposition triggers carry propositions of some necessary and sufficient conditions which determine whether events described in the texts of the American University Alma Mater and Fight Song took place. The main statements of the authors of the songs can thus be looked upon as statements about whether the decisive conditions they envisioned for generating the texts were fulfilled, and under what spatial and temporal circumstances.

This is good to know because these presupposition triggers indicate the sort of range of presuppositional phenomena the authors of the songs had. This set of core phenomena will make it possible for the examination in future research of some further basic properties that the authors' presuppositions exhibit.

Endnotes

1. Interested readers can find greater details in Bangura (2000, 1997 & 1996), Bangura and Thomas (1998), Gazdar (1997), and Levinson (1983).

2. *Modus ponens* refers to the inference $p \rightarrow q$ and $\sim p$ to $\sim q$.

3. *Bivalence* refers to the assumption $pv \sim p$) that a presupposition must be either true or false.

4. *Modus tollens* refers to the inference from $p \rightarrow q$ and $q \sim$ to $\sim p$.

5. *Deictic context* refers to the speech event in which languages encode or grammaticalize linguistic features. The traditional categories of deixis are person, place, and time (Levinson 1983:54, 62). To these traditional categories, Lyons (1977) and Filmore (1968, 1975) added discourse (or text) deixis and social deixis.

Chapter 6

Implicatures

The notion of linguistic implicature does not have an extensive history like presupposition or many other topics in pragmatics. The idea of implicature can be traced back to Grice's (1975, 1978) theory of conversational implicature.[1] This theory, according to Grice (1975:45), is derived from a general principle of conversation called the *cooperative principle* plus a number of maxims which speakers will normally obey.

The term implicature, as used by Grice, accounts for what a speaker (or a writer) can imply, suggest, or mean, as distinguished from what the speaker (or the writer) literally says (or writes). Linguistic implicatures, Grice suggested, are determined by "the conventional meaning of the words used" (1975:44).

Implicature is, therefore, an important unit of linguistic analysis for at least five reasons, following Levinson (1983:97-100). First, the concept of implicature offers some significant functional explanations of linguistic facts because the sources of this concept can be shown to lie outside the organization of language, in some general principles for cooperative interaction. And yet the principles have a pervasive effect upon the structure of language. This makes implicature a paradigmatic example of the nature and power of pragmatic explanations of linguistic phenomena.

Second, implicature provides some explicit account of how it is possible to mean more than what is actually said or written. Put differently, the concept allows an analyst to identify more than what is literally expressed by the conventional sense of the linguistic expressions uttered or written. Consider the following example:

(1) A: What time will George Bush address the nation?

B: Most people watch television during the national evening news.

All that can be reasonably expected employing semantic theory in analyzing this small example is that there is at least one reading that can be paraphrased as follows:

(2) A: Do you have the ability to tell me the time George Bush will address the nation?

B: Most people watch television during the national evening news which comes on between 7:00 pm and 7:30 pm.

Yet it is clear to native English speakers that what would ordinarily be communicated by such an exchange involves considerably more, along the lines of the material in (3).

(3) A: Do you have the ability to tell me the time George Bush will address the nation, as standardly indicated on a watch, and if so please do so tell me.

B: No I don't know the exact time George Bush will address the nation, but I can provide some information from which you may be able to deduce the approximate time George Bush is more likely to reach the largest audience, namely during the national evening news which comes on between 7:00 pm and 7:30 pm.

Third, implicature seems likely to effect substantial simplifications in both the structure and the content of semantic descriptions, as the following example shows.

(4) On his way to becoming President of the United States, Lyndon Johnson won the Democratic presidential nomination by a smaller margin and won the national presidential election by a landslide.

(5) The vice presidential candidate for the Republican Party is Dan Quayle and the vice presidential candidate for the Democratic Party is Lloyd Bentsen.

(6) ?? On his way to becoming President of the United States, Lyndon Johnson won the national presidential election by a landslide and won the Democratic presidential nomination by a smaller margin.

(7) The vice presidential candidate for the Democratic Party is Lloyd Bentsen and the vice presidential candidate for the Republican Party is Dan Quayle.

The sense of *and* in (4) and (5) appear to be rather different: in (4) it appears to mean 'and then' and, therefore, (6) appears strange in the sense that a candidate must first win his party nomination before winning a national presidential election on his way to becoming President of the United States. But in (5) there is no 'and then' sense; *and* here seems to mean just what the standard truth table for & would have it mean—that is, the whole is true just in case both conjuncts are true;

hence, the reversal of the conjuncts in (7) does not affect the conceptual import at all. For the semanticist, the two distinct senses of the word *and* can be declared simply ambiguous, or it can be claimed that the meanings of words are, in general, vague and protean and are influenced by collocational environments.

Fourth, the notion of implicature seems to be essential when various basic facts about language are to be accounted for properly. For example, particles like *well* and *by the way* require some meaning specification in a theory of meaning just like other words in English; but when a linguist comes to consider what their meaning is, s/he will find her/himself referring to the pragmatic mechanisms that produce implicatures.

Finally, the principles that generate implicatures possess a very general explanatory power in the sense that a few basic principles provide explanations for a large array of apparently unrelated facts. Examples suggested and discussed by Levinson (1983:100-166) include why English has no lexical item *nall,* meaning 'not all,' why Aristotle got his logic wrong, 'Moore's paradox,' how obvious tautologies like *War is war* can convey any conceptual import, and how metaphors work and many other phenomena besides.

Grice (1975) suggested that the essential properties of implicatures are largely predictable. He isolated four characteristic properties that can be employed to test for implicatures. These characteristic properties are: (a) *cancellability* or *defeasibility*, (b) *non-detachability*, (c) *calculability*, and (d) *non-conventionality*. A possible fifth characteristic property of implicature can be referred to as "multiplicity"—that is, what Levinson (1983:117-118) referred to as "an expression with a single meaning (which) can give rise to different implicatures on different occasions, and indeed on any one occasion the set of associated implicatures may not be exactly determinable" (Levinson attributed this definition to Wilson and Sperber 1981).

The Projection Problem

The projection problem for implicatures—that is, the implicatures of complex expressions may not be equivalent to the simple sum of the implicatures of all parts—exists because of a number of different kinds of *Quantity implicature* such as *clausal* and *scalar*. Consider the following example in which the implicature can be suspended by explicit mention in *if*-clauses.

(8) Some, if not all, the Founding Fathers owned slaves.

Here, there should be a scalar implicature (9) due to *some* (by the rule for deriving scalar implicatures[2]).

(9) K~(all the Founding Fathers owned slaves)
i.e. S knows that not all the Founding Fathers owned slaves.

But there should also be the clausal implicature (10) due to the phrase if *not all*:[3]

(10) P(all the Founding fathers owned slaves)
i.e. it is possible, for all S knows, that all of the Founding Fathers owned slaves.

Now the two implicatures (9) and (10) are inconsistent, and it is clear that the clausal implicature (10) effectively cancels the scalar implicature (9).

Examples such as these led Gazdar (1979) to set up a projection (or cancellation) mechanism designed to model implicature cancellation. Levinson (1983:143) stated Gazdar's projection mechanism more succinctly as follows:

Let the communicative content of an utterance U be assessed by adding the distinct semantic and pragmatic inferences of U sequentially to the context C, where C is understood to be the set of beliefs that the speaker is committed to at the point when U is uttered. On the utterance of U, first the *entailments* (or semantic content) of U are added to the context. Next, all the *clausal* implicatures are added that are *consistent* with the content of C, inconsistent clausal implicatures simply being rejected and not added to the set of propositions in context C. Only now can *scalar* implicatures be added, just in case they in turn are consistent with the context as already incremented by the entailments and clausal implicature of U.

On this account, *defeasibility* is also captured by making implicatures acceptable only if they are consistent with entailments and other implicatures that have priority. Gazdar's mechanism also explains where implicatures may be overtly denied as in the following sentence:

(11) Some politicians receive money from Political Action Committees, in fact probably all.

Here, the entailments of the second clause, being added to the context of the first, will cancel the implicature due to *some*.

Thus, all an analyst needs to do, according to Levinson (1983:144), is to refine his or her understanding of *non-detachability* as follows: "implicatures will be preserved by the substitution of synonymous expressions provided that the substitutes carry no additional implicatures or entailments inconsistent with the original expressions (and which happen to have priority in the incremental mechanism outlined [by Gazdar]").

It is clear from the preceding discussion that implicature plays a major role in analyzing changes (both syntactic and semantic) in the texts of the American University Alma Mater and Fight Song examined for this book. The concept serves as an important mechanism for understanding how matters of language usage (of the composers of the songs analyzed) feed back into and affect matters of language structure. Implicature, as a unit of linguistic analysis in this book is, thus, a major route for explaining functional historical pressures that left their imprint on the structure of language at the time the songs were composed.

Implicatures in the Songs

Existing in the American University Alma Mater and Fight Song are the following implicatures:

(12) College years are expected to pass.

(13) Days that fly past are usually recalled.

(14) Days are usually treasured and lived in.

(15) People usually yearn for the pleasures of college.

(16) Friendships are expected to bind and remind people of school colors.

(17) Days are expected to be fullest in measure.

(18) Everyone is expected to hail the American University Eagles (athletic teams).

(19) Fights ought to be seen through.

(20) One ought to be sure to be triumphant.

(21) Red, white and blue colors are usually worn.

(22) Enemies are usually conquered.

(23) Everyone is expected to join in and yell for American University to be victorious.

These implicatures are triggered by the following implicative predicates: "soon behind," "recalling days," "year now," "bind,"…and "remind," "come days," "hail the mighty," "'ll see," "can be sure," "when we wear," "'ll conquer," and "join and give a yell," respectively. As stated in the previous chapter, implicative predicates carry presuppositions that reflect a necessary and sufficient condition for the truth of their complement sentences. As also noted in that chapter, an asserted main sentence with an implicative verb commits the writer/speaker to an implied proposition which consists of a complement sentence as augmented by the tense and other modifiers of the main sentence.

In the preceding analysis, I have somehow limited the number of possible implicatures that can be delineated from the songs. This is because the implications one can draw from some act are much broader than meaning in natural language. There is also a real danger based on the fact that a contradiction implies anything and everything. All self-contradictory concepts must have precisely the same meaning, namely everything. Unfortunately, the theory of implicature has not yet developed limits to prevent this.

Endnotes

1. Levinson (1983:100n), however, noted that there was considerable speculation within philosophy about the utility of the notion of pragmatic implication, and some proto-Gricean ideas appear in Fogelin (1967).

2. The rule for deriving *scalar implicatures* from the scalar predicates is as follows: Given any scale of the form $<e_1, e_2, e_3,...e_n>$, if a speaker asserts $A(e_2)$, then s/he implicates $\sim A(e_1)$, if s/he asserts $A(e_3)$, then s/he implicates $\sim A(e_2)$ and $\sim A(e_1)$, and in general, if s/he asserts $A(e_n)$, then s/he implicates $\sim (A(e_n-1))$, $\sim (A(e_n-2)$ and so on, up to $\sim (A(e_1))$. For the scalar implicature to be actually inferred, the expression that gives rise to it must be entailed, thus, by any complex sentence of which it is a part (Levinson 1983:133).

3. The predicate of *clausal implicatures* of 'if p then q' is the following:
$$\{Pp, P\sim p, Pq \ P\sim q\}$$

Chapter 7

Speech Acts

This chapter is about the speech acts in the texts of the American University Alma Mater and Fight Song. First, a synopsis about the theory is presented. Second, a more detailed discussion of the works of the pioneers of the theory is provided. Finally, the speech acts in the American University Alma Mater and Fight Song are discussed.

Speech Act Theory postulates that the utterance of certain sentences, must, in special environments, be seen as the performance of an act, either direct or indirect. The notion of speech acts can be traced to the works of two major linguistic philosophers: J. L. Austin (1962) and J. R. Searle (1969).

In 1962, Austin observed that, while sentences can often be used to report state of affairs, the utterance of some sentences, in special cases, are to be treated as the performance of an act. Such sentences, suggested Austin, can be called *Performatives*, and the special circumstances required for their success, he referred to as *a set of felicity conditions*. By extension, Austin proposed that in uttering any sentence (a *Locutionary Act*), a speaker can be seen to have performed some act (an *Illocutionary Act*). Associated with each illocutionary act is the *Force* of the utterance that can be interpreted as a performative like "promise," "warn," etc. Austin also pointed out that, in uttering a sentence, a speaker also performs a

Perlocutionary Act, which is described in terms of the effect the illocutionary act, at the particular time in use, has on the hearer.

Seven years later (1969), Searle introduced a variation between *direct* and *indirect* speech acts which depends on a recognition of the intended perlocutionary effect of an utterance on a given occasion. For Searle, indirect speech acts are cases in which one illocutionary act is performed indirectly by way of performing another. To support this proposition, he provided his now famous example, "Can you pass the salt?," and proposed two ways it can be interpreted: (1) it can be seen as a question about the hearer's *ability* to pass the salt; (2) it can be interpreted as a *request* for the action of passing the salt.

The use of Speech Act Theory in studying language phenomena is, thus, important because it provides an account of how some apparently formally unconnected statements go together in discourse to form a coherent sequence. However, there is a general problem with such an approach, and it has been pointed out by Levinson as follows: "If one looks even curiously at a transcribed record of a conversation, it becomes immediately clear that we do not know how to assign speech acts in a non-arbitrary way" (1980:20).

More concretely, Leech (1983:207-8) has pointed out two aspects of the problem. The first aspect is that of polysemy: i.e. some verbs are so versatile that they can fit both syntactically and semantically into more than one category. For instance, *advise, suggest,* and *tell* can either be classified as assertive or directive. Thus, according to Leech, our classification should not be so much a classification of verbs, but one of verb SENSES.

The second aspect, according to Leech, is that certain verbs, such as *greet* (which is simply followed by a direct object), do not take clausal complementizers, although semantically they must imply one. To solve this shortcoming, Leech suggested that the analyst could do what Searle suggested by stipulating that the syntactic frames that go with each verb category are 'deep structures' which may appear in surface structure in various disguises. Leech also suggested that the analyst can replace the 'deep structure' analysis by an analysis at the semantic representation level, where one is "no longer concerned with speech-act verbs, but rather with the speech-act PREDICATES which they realize, and where the reported utterance is represented by a metapropositional argument" (Leech 1983:208).

Moreover, as Brown and Yule also have argued:

> The problem with identifying speech acts should not necessarily lead the analyst to abandon their investigation. Rather, it should lead the analyst to recognize that the way speech acts are conventionally classified into discrete act-types such as 'request,' 'promise,' 'warn,' etc. may lead to an inappropriate view of what speakers do with utterances (1978:233).

What solidifies this axiom (i.e. Speech Acts Theory), despite the fact that it had been traditionally subsumed under the rubric of *Theoretical Linguistics*, is the notion of *Sociolinguistics*: i.e. the desire to capture how languages are embedded in the surrounding frameworks of cultures and social institutions.

Austin and Searle

'Acts' demand responsible choice, 'Processes' merely occur, and 'States' are just there. Language viewed as Systematic options with Structural consequences metaphorically specifies possible 'intentions' for the Ideal Speaker-Hearer—a kind of being readily conceivable but never found in experience. Actual intentions of actual speakers are dubiously objects of any science. But with Hjlemslev's Denotative versus Connotative Semiotic distinction, some metaphoric traps are avoidable. Studies of Conditions on Speech Acts show why this is so.

Symbols are distinguishable internally within their peculiar system by opposition, externally by connexity with the nonsymbolic: de Saussure's negative *Value* and positive *Signification*, interpretable in his peculiar use of *Content* as their logical sum or union. The vocabulary used by Austin, or any specialist, should be viewed from that perspective: partial identity in signification—what a sign refers to—can obscure differences in value, therefore differences in total content.

The Saussurean signification-value content triad provides a framework for comparing vocabularies about what Hjelmslev neutrally labeled 'purport'—vaguely, what is somehow 'meant'— partitionable from different vantage points, for different purposes. Austin contrasted *performative* utterances with *constative* ones, and built his theory of Speech Acts on the difference. Case Grammar's system opposes nominal Agential (A) to active or passive Experiential (E) Roles, and both to Objective (O) and Instrumental (I), Beneficial (B), or Locative (L) ones. Deliberate Speech (S) essentially concerns Experiential Roles, productive and receptive. So it is of particular interest to examine the extent to which *Act* in Austin's conception and *Action* in Case Grammar coincide and idffer.

Austin took a *Locutionary* Speech Act to be the speaker's act of saying what he says: it can be provisionally viewed as Case Grammar's relation of an O to its A. An *Illocutionary* Speech Act is one performed *in* uttering something: provisionally, the productive E of the O produced by A. A *Perlocutionary* Speech Act is one we perform simply *by* saying something: provisionally, this involves at least the E receptive of the O produced by an A. When E is neither productively nor receptively focused, a nonlinguistic, non-experiential, nonpropositional O (an 'outer O, which itself may be an S'). Can be involved, in which case the utterance would be treated as a Modal, a kind of nonexperiential Instrument.

How to Do Things with Words

Austin's slender book was reconstructed from his extensive notes by his Oxford friend and colleague, J. O. Urmson. Austin wrote that the ideas found in it were forming in 1939, had been presented in stages as 'Other Minds' (Proceedings of the Aristotelian Society Supplement Vol. XX. 1946) and as the Oxford 'Words and Deeds' lectures he revised for the 1955 Harvard series.

Lecture I distinguishes overt sentences from convert statements: sentences are not, but may be used to make, true or false statements. When empirical evidence is required to verify them, the process unmasks empirical pseudo-statements: so ethical propositions, for instance, rank empirically as emotive, rather than empirically descriptive reports. To mistake emotive for descriptive terms was labelled a *Descriptive* Fallacy, for which Austin preferred the term *constative*, in order to contrast it first with *performative*. Constatives are statements with 'historical' reference, while Performatives are not. When uttering a Performative, one thereby 'performs' an action, and is not just saying something (e.g., in 'I declare war' or 'I bet you,' 'I give you'). But without an appropriate frame (authority, seriousness, completion, reciprocity), speakers do not really 'perform,' verbally or otherwise. Presupposition failure can render performance void—but not false, in Austin's view—except perhaps in the case of promises.

Lecture II recapitulates basic distinctions. American legal rules of evidence disallow descriptive reports as 'hearsay'; but if they involve performatives, they are admissable as evidence of 'acts' (e.g., overt promises or threats). When things go wrong in performatives, it seems more appropriate to speak of *infelicity* rather than falsity. Things can 'go wrong' when conventional frames are wanting or inappropriate, when participation is incomplete, wanting in intent, or later conduct.

At this stage of Austin's study, the problem is taxonomic and terminological. Austin's scheme lays out these contrasts (18):

Infelicities

AB	GAMMA
Misfires	Abuses
Act purported but void but hollow	Act professed

A	B	G_1	G_2
Misinvocations	Misexecutions	Insincerities	?
Act disallowed	Act vitiated		

A_1	A_2	B_1	B_2
?	Misapplic-ations	Flaws	Hitches

Since Searle would later focus on the problem of what the constituents intimately involved are, and how best to label them, Austin's formulation of it at this point is worth quoting:

(1) To what variety of 'act' does the notion of infelicity apply?
(2) How complete is this classifications of infelicity?
(3) Are these classes of infelicity mutually exclusive?

Conventional rituals and ceremonies come under (1): wills, deeds, and wagers. Purported statements about nonexistent bald kings of France (like leaving what you don't possess in a will) are better viewed as void than false. Under (2), the first thing to notice is that, as performances, actions are generally free of duress, accident, mistake or want of intention (e.g., accidental killing as opposed to murder). Secondly, as utterance, stimulation (like actors' portrayal of passions they do not genuinely feel) or misunderstanding (by children or foreigners) is excluded in the case of promises. Since gradience and overlap are common here, Austin thought (3) has to be answered in the negative: e.g., invalid christening of ships, or valid but unauthorized weddings, or saints baptizing penguins.

Lecture III takes up A_1: the need for existent, accepted, conventional procedure, effect, verbalization, participants and circumstances. One player's 'You're out!' does not suffice to render another player 'out': that is the prerogative of umpires. What does 'I'm not playing' do to 'I pick you,' or 'You can't order me' to 'Stop that!' under A_1 or B_2? Acceptance can turn on degrees of *explicitness*: this may range from the use of the explicitly performative verb *order*, through imperative forms, to oblique or ambiguous reports, asides, or questions softening what could be legitimately demanded.

A_2 concerns appropriate persons and circumstances, relevant capacities and occasions (e.g., the effect of bigamous 'I dos,' Captain's 'man and wife' ashore, the promising of evils, misnaming infants, electing a horse Consul, etc.). B_1 treats flaws in procedure, word or persons; B_2 deals with faulty participation ('No bet,' 'I do not take her as wife,' a ship-launch before 'I christen thee' has been uttered). Simplicity is not to be preferred to Exhaustiveness in this kind of study.

Lecture IV takes up Gamma 1 and 2 about sincerity before and during a procedure, confirmable by behavior after it. Examples involve perfunctory congratulations and condolences (Phatic Communion?), expedient excuse or verdict, and bravado in bet or threat. These can be complicated by false information, mitigating circumstances, explicit but bad advice, or questionable verdicts (e.g., the perennial 'blind' umpire's 'Out!'). Subsequence complications: failure to follow through on gifts, promises and sales; velleity (sincere but implemented wish), and pro forma invitations (like 'Stop in and see us when you're in Washington').

Performatives differ from constatives (a) in being in the first person, present, non-progressive and declarative, while (b) constatives are not so limited; (c) constatives are true or false in what they assert; performatives, like 'I apologize,' by what they do (saying 'I run' is true if in fact I run; saying 'I apologize,' if I do so under the conditions of the Gamma 1 and 2). (d) Since the distinction is between doing and saying, while constatives can *be* true statements, performatives strictly speaking *imply* them.

Austin then distinguished *entail, imply* and *presuppose* as mentioned above, stressing that these do not involve *contradictions* (which is a different and more complex determination). But if I don't believe the cat is on the mat and say so anyway, *sincerity* is as lacking as in facile invitations, or 'I promise but have no intention of....' Denying jack's children exist after asserting that they are bald is neither false nor meaningless, but *void*, like the marital contract what A-conditions are absent or ambiguous, despite 'I do.'

Actions have consequences, so 'I promise' entails *'ought'*: to attempt a promise and simultaneously live 'ought not' both commit you to it and refuses to commit you to it. Concentrating on propositions is insufficient to tell what can go wrong in the total situation of their use.

Lecture V sums up IV by relating performative utterances and statements determinately true or false: (1) if 'I apologize' is felicitous, then the statement 'I am apologizing' is true; (2) if felicitous, then statements that Rules A and B hold are true; (3) if felicitous, then Rule Gamma 1 must be true, and (4) if others (like contractuals) are felicitous, then 'oughts' for later behaviour are true.

Austin found (2) for Performatives about identicals to what are called Presuppositions for statements, although he doubted the identity is that strong for (3) when identified as Implications. A strong connection, yes, but not the kind demanded 'by obsessional logicians' (1962:54). Perhaps (4) qualifies. Does this confuse things? The statement 'John is running' may have involved a higher performative like '*I state* that John is running,' just as 'I am apologizing' depends on '*I apologize*'; 'I warn you the bull's about to charge' may be sincere, but quite mistaken. Is there a linguistic basis for the performative/constative distinction?

Sly 'classic' 1st person, indicative, etc. overts like 'I name.' 'I bet' can be deceptive–they can be generic; the grammarians' *indicative* (as report or description), or *present* tense versus *habitual* aspect hardly describes performatives aptly. Austin thought that Latin *curro* should be 'I am running' which is *indicative*, since he said that Latin lacks a ± progressive contrast. (This is incomplete: the Latin imperfect *currebam* is progressive and past; present perfect *cuccurri* is past, but not progressive (FPD).

Included as Performatives are 2nd person 'You are hereby authorized…,' 3rd person 'Passengers are warned…,' and impersonal 'Notice is hereby given….' So *hereby* is a useful criterion for identifying performatives: if the normal expression can contain 'I hereby…,' it is an explicit performative. But criteria involving mood and tense break down quickly: 'Turn right' is equivalent to 'I order you to turn right,' 'You should' is like 'I advise,' and 'You were out' and 'You are out' are as final as 'You did it' or 'I find you guilty.' 'Done!' is as binding as 'I hereby accept your wager.' Ellipsis is as normal as abbreviation, so no single lexical or grammatical device serves infallibly to mark performatives: there are *asymmetries* between words and acts. (1) Present indicative can be habitual, (2) or historic progressive, (3) or serve two functions at once; (4) could involve nonperformatives (e.g., 'I state' vs 'I bet'), (5) action suits the word ('I checkmate,' 'I spit'); (6) some lack explicit verbs ('I hereby insult'), and (7) paraphrase can make some *inexplicit*.

VI pursues a performative/constative distinction: no positive grammatical or lexical basis uniquely defines it. Their gradient differences might be helped by contrasting (1) *primary* versus (2) *explicit* performatives, where (1) could be 'I'll be there' and (2) 'I promise that I shall be there': of the first (but not reasonably of the second) one could inquire about promissory status—'Does that mean you promise?'

Adding 'Salaam' to a low bow neither reports nor truly/falsely describes my ceremonial act. Subordination by ('I promise) *that*,' as in indirect discourse, is obscure, and not absolutely required. Austin thought (citing Jespersen) that current preformatives ought to be relics of 'original' one-word utterances: they were initially obscure, and later sophistication in clarifying them 'is as much a creative act as a discovery or description' (1962:72).

Philosophers' assumption of a 'pure statement' obscures this: clarification is not making explicit a statement's *meaning* but its *force* (how it is to be taken). Explicitating performatives is only the last and most successful speech-device, comparable to standard measurements for *precision* in language. Other primitive devices might be supplanted by performatives. The following are examples:

(1) *Mood:*   *Resembles:*

Shut it	I order you to shut it
Shut it—I should	I advise you to shut it
Shut it, if you like	I permit you to shut it
Very well then, shut it	I consent to your shutting it
Shut it, if you dare	I dare you to shut it
You may shut it	I give permission, consent to shutting it
You must shut it	I order, advise, you to shut it
You ought to shut it	I advise you to shut it

(2) *Tone, cadence, emphasis:*

It's going to CHARGE !	warning
It's going to CHARGE ?	question
It's going to CHARGE ?	protest

(3) *Adverb(ials)*:

'I shall (probably) ... (without fail) ...' 'You would do well never to forget that...have to do with phenomena of '...evincing, intimating, insinuation, innuendo, giving to understand, enabling to infer, conveying, 'expressing' (odious word)...' (1962:75).

(4) *Connecting particles*:

Use of particles like 'still' for 'I insist that' or 'therefore' for 'I conclude that' or 'whereas,' 'hereby,' 'moreover' and the like are comparable to the words like Manifesto, Act, Decree, or the subheading 'A Novel...' can clarify performative status, but it raises the question again about the performative status of 'I conclude' and 'I concede that.' Performatives are also explicitated by

(5) *Accompaniments*:

(E.g., shrugs, frowns, winks...)

(6) *Circumstances of the utterance*:

'Coming from him, I took it as an order, not a request,' 'When I die...' and other such expressions stress the inherent vagueness of meaning. So these and combinations of others are required. When clear performatives do exist, they can be used in formulae other than 'I × that' or 'I × to,' which are almost diagnostic of their status (e.g., stage directions, parentheses, titles).

But there are still problems about apparently explicit performatives:

(1) they can be mistaken for constatives or descriptives in philosophy
(1a) when dubious in either direction
(2) clear formulae are subject to varied use, e.g.:

I thank	I am grateful	I feel grateful
I apologize	I am sorry	I repent
I criticize		I am shocked by
I blame		
I censure		I am revolted by
I approve	I approve of	I feel approval
I bid you welcome	I welcome	
I congratulate	I am glad about	

Those in the first column are good performatives, the second are semis, and the third are dubious. One test: 'Does he really?'; another, doing without saying (e.g., blaming versus censuring); a third, 'can deliberately' or 'I am willing to' be inserted; a fourth, whether falsity or insincerity would be involved.

An uncertainty attaches to *polite* phrases like 'I have the honor to...'; to expressions 'suiting the action to the word' (salute, salaam), to transitionals like 'Snap,' 'Check,' 'I quote,' 'I define': are these titles or performatives?

Lecture VI deals with BEHABATIVES (Austin knew it's a strange word to coin, but hr found it useful to characterize performatives involved in reactions to behavior. Lecture VII takes us to EXPOSITIVES: these mainly involve a statement, but with an explicit performative to show how it is to be taken. The following are examples:

I argue (or urge)
I conclude (or infer)

I testify that there is no backside to the moon
I admit (or concede)
I prophesy (or predict)

These tests gather different results: i.e., 'was he *really* (arguing, testifying etc.'; doing without saying; deliberately; true-falsely or insincerely). Besides, afterthoughts allow us to say without dishonesty. 'Of course, I was assuming that…' and 'thus' provide a fine line between feeling and statement or judgements. Similarly, 'I postulate that' is a pure explicit performative, while 'I assume that' is not, and 'I imply that' or 'insinuate that' are not performatives at all for Austin.

This distinction of what can and cannot be done with explicit performatives and BEHABATIVES and EXPOSITIVES is paralleled in another class which he called VERDICTIVES: official (versus private) judgements like 'I deem,' 'I hold,' 'I find,' 'I pronounce': here, the status depends on circumstances, not just on language. The problem being discussed here is whether 'an apparent or suggested explicit performative verb itself operates, or operates sometimes or in part, as a description, true or false, of feelings, states of mind, frames of mind, etc.' (1962:89). To say that such usage by nonofficials has no true/false standing (i.e. as statements about facts) is as oversharp as Caterpillar's critique of Alice (who began 'I don't think…'), 'Then you shouldn't talk,' since the opening tells how what follows is to be taken.

Austin summarized his position at this point (1962:90): distinguishing performative and constative utterances, it is clear that both have felicity conditions, and that even performatives have somehow to conform to facts; surface forms are never unambiguously performatives, and even explicit ones serve varied uses. He then proposed 'a fresh start' on clarifying the senses in which 'to say something is to do something,' or in saying something we do something (and perhaps the different case in which *by* saying something we do something): but 'action' is vague, as is the contrast between men of words and men of action, those who *do* and those who only *talk*. He wants to refine the circumstances of issuing an utterance'—hence Class A: to say anything is:

(A.a)   always to perform the act of uttering certain noises (a 'phonetic act') and the utterance is a *'phone'*;

(A.b)   always to perform the act of uttering certain vocables or words, i.e. noises of certain types as belonging to a certain vocabulary, in a certain construction, i.e. comforming to and as comforming to a certain grammar, with a certain intonation, etc. This act we may call a *'phatic'* act, and the utterance which it is the act of uttering a *'pheme'* (as distinct from the phememe of linguistic theory); and

(A.c)   generally to perform the act of using the pheme or its constituents with a certain more or less definite 'sense' and a more or less definite 'reference' (which together are equivalent to 'meaning'). This act we may call a *'rhetic' act* and the utterance which it is the act of uttering a *'rheme.'*

Lecture VIII calls the 'act of saying something' in this full normal sense the PERFORMANCE of a LOCUTIONARY act, and the study of utterances so far, and in these respects, the study of LOCUTIONS, or of the full units of speech. Also to be distinguished are the phonetic acts (phonation), phatic acts (in a language) and rhetic acts (with sense and reference). So 'He said "the cat is on the mat"' reports a phatic act; 'He said that the cat was on the mat' reports a rhetic act, and parallel distinctions hold among:

'He said "I shall be there"'
    & 'He said he would be there'

'He said "Get out"'
   & 'He told me to get out'
'He said "Is it in Oxford or Cambridge?"'
   & 'He asked whether it was in Oxford or Cambridge'

Note that (1) phatic acts are phonetic, but the relation is asymmetrical; (2) vocabulary and lexicon were not distinguished, so nonsense is not yet accounted for; and (3) while phatic or phonetic acts can be mimicked, the rhetic act is what we report. Austin equated *sense* with *naming*, and *reference* with *referring*, and suggested that they are ancillary in rhetic acts. He found puzzling cases of rhetic acts without reference (e.g., he asks what's the reference in 'All triangles have three sides.' ?). He also points out that we can repeat others' remarks or foreign texts without knowing the meaning.

There are other puzzles not directly dealt with: when phemes and rhemes are 'the same' (as types or tokens); how identified phemes can be used for different sense or reference and so be different rhemes; or when different phemes are used as rhetically equivalent. But the pheme is s unit of *language* and its typical fault is that it can be nonsense, while the rheme is a unit of *speech* whose typical fault is to be vague, void or obscure. Such problems are not dealt with because they do not illuminate his central problem, but they provide occasion to stress that to perform a locutionary act is in general also *eo ipso* to perform an *illocutionary* act (asking, answering, informing, judging, sentencing, criticizing, describing, identifying, etc). But these demand subdistinctions, such as advising versus suggesting, promising or tending toward: these are problems not grammatically decidable, and the proper form for questioning them has to do with whether words, for example, *had the force of* a question, or whether they *ought to have been taken as* an estimate, etc.: in short, the performance of an act *in* saying something versus the performance of an act *of* saying something, hence the study of 'illocutionary forces.'

Austin intended to refine the distinction of 'descriptive fallacy' (confusing reactions with factual report). And just as 'meaning' is profitably divided into sense and reference, he wanted to distinguish *force* from *meaning*, particularly where 'meaning' was to be resolved into that of words, since it is increasingly apparent that the occasion of an utterance matters seriously.

'Use' of language is as hopelessly vague a term as 'meaning,' which it was supposed to supplant. Having distinguished an *A* sense of 'act' and a *B* sense (the way versus the sense in which we 'use' it) we need a *C* sense, combining a locutionary and illocutionary act for yet another (e.g., affecting others). For example:

(E.1)

    Act (A)   or   Locution

        he said to me 'Shoot her' meaning by 'shoot' shoot and referring by 'her' to *her*.

    Act (B)   or   Illocution

        He urged (or advised, ordered, etc.) me to shoot her.

    Act (C.a)   or   Perlocution

        He persuaded me to shoot her.

    Act (C.b)

        He got me (or made me, etc.) shoot her.

(E.2)

    Act (A)   or   Locution

        He said to me, 'You can't do that.'

    Act (B)   or   Illocution

        He protested against my doing it.

Act (C.a)   or   Perlocution
    He pulled me up, checked me.

Act (C.b)
    He stopped me, he brought me to my senses, etc.
    He annoyed me.

We can also distinguish the locutionary act, 'he said that,' from the illocutionary act, 'he argued that,' and the perlocutionary act, 'he convinced me that....' Differences among them include their *consequences*, such as lack of conventional commitment of the speaker. This returned Austin to some points about the 'use' of language:

(1) Concentration on locution or perlocution rather than illocution is confused by concentration *on both* 'meaning' and 'use.' The three are distinct. One reason is the lack of conventionality: we say and make explicit 'I argue that,' but not 'I convince you that' or 'I alarm you that.'

(2) There are 'uses' of language which have nothing to do with an illocutioary act, e.g. joking, poetry: one can speak of 'a poetical use of language' as distinct from 'the use of language in poetry'; there are parasitic uses of language where normal conditions of reference are suspended and no perlocutioanry act is attempted (e.g., Walt Whitman's poetry).

(3) There are things we 'do' which seem to escape these classifications, such as insinuating, or evincing emotion: one can say we use swearing *for* relieving emotions, but an illocutionary act is a *conventional* act.

(4) We are imperfect and so are our acts, so we have to distinguish between doing, achieving, and attempting x.

(5) Effects can be intended or unintended, may follow or fail to occur, as provided for under (4). We often disambiguate with 'unintentionally.'

(6) We also have to allow for cases of duress, in which we cannot be said to *do* things in the same sense.

(7) We think physically about 'acts': we need a conventional, as well as a consequential, perspective.

   (a) illocutionary and locutionary acts are subject to conventions (compare kicking a ball and kicking a goal);

   (b) consequences of perlocutionary acts cannot be restricted-physically, but this is a peculiarity of 'action' in general. We can resort to a formula like '*by* B-ing he C-ed' rather than '*in* B-ing....' That is why he called C a *per*locutionary act as distinct from *il*locutionary.

Lecture IX takes up the need to distinguish 'Consequences.' Since any act of any kind has consequences, this fact alone cannot distinguish performatives from constatives. So we have to draw a line between illocution and its consequences. Acts are generally defined in terms of consequences; but (1) from the *nomenclature* for physical acts compared to speech acts, we seem to have an advantage: names for speech acts seem expressly designed to mark a break between act and consequence; (2) physical acts have at least physical consequences, but speech acts may not have further speech as consequences, and uttering words is not the same as just making noise; the reference involved in the speaking of words is not to physical things, but conventions of illocutionary force, bearing on circumstances and occasions of utterance.

So Austin argued that "we can have hopes of isolating the illocutioanry act from the perlocutionary as producing consequences, and that it is not itself a 'consequence' of the locutionary act" (1962:115). But a felicitous illocutionary act must have its own kind of effect: warnings must be heard and appreciated as warnings. Austin termed this a matter of (1) *uptake*: meaning and force are understood. (2) 'Taking effect' is different from producing consequences; e.g., later calling the *Queen Elizabeth I* the *Stalin* is out of order. (3) 'Getting someone to X' by an illocutionary act is distinct from a perlocutionary act, for which the speaker is responsible.

Austin proposed the distinction of achieving perlocutionary objects like conviction and persuasion from producing perlocutionary sequels, like trying to warn, but succeeding in alarming. There are perlocutionary acts lacking objects, but with sequels, so there is no illocutionary formula for 'I surprise...upset...humiliate you by....' Perlocutionary effects can almost all be attained by nonlinguistic means, but what is more important is whether they can be accomplished nonconventionally: strictly speaking, there cannot be an illocutionary act unless the means employed are conventional—but how can we know where they begin and where they end?

Lecture X stresses that perlocutionary acts are *not* conventional, although conventional acts may be employed to attain their results. Judges should be able to determine, not what perlocutionary acts were achieved, but what locutionary and ilocutionary acts were performed. Austin then wrote about other ways of 'using' language, summarized in the dollowing formulae:

| 'In saying | x | I was doing y' | or | 'I did y' |
| 'By saying | x | I did y' | or | 'I was doing y' |

as in joking, non-literal or nonserious uses, showing off, emotive uses, etc. The possibility of such formulae suggested the name to him:

*il*locutionary: '*In* saying I would shoot him, I was threatening him.'

*per*locutionary: '*By* saying I would shoot him, I alarmed him.'

But these formulae alone are no test for distinguishing ILLOCUTIONARY ACTS from PERLOCUTIONARY ACTS. So Austin asked, 'Why not cut the cackle' and get straight to psychology and linguistics? (1962:122). We could not because it would be to go too fast, and we would overlook things clued by language.

Comparing the formulae, 'In saying x I was doing y (or did y)' applies locutionary acts and acts outside of Austin's classification. It at least does not fit perlocutioanry acts; it doesn't exclude a 'by' formulation, does not fit the illocutionary. Or one might object that 'saying' is ambiguous, and that the range of vocabulary fitting it has not been sufficiently determined: e.g., is 'argue' always 'try to convince,' or 'warn,' 'try to alert,' or 'alarm'? Recall the distinction of trying and doing, and the fact that one can promise not to try to do anything.

Another way of proceeding is to assume that the 'in' of the formula involves saying A, doing B; where A involves or accounts for B, or vice versa: e.g., in building a house/I was building a wall; in saying A/I was forgetting B; in buzzing/I was thinking that butterflies buzzed; in buzzing/I was pretending to be a bee; in buzzing / I was behaving like a buffoon.

The 'by' formula is not confined to perlocutionaries: pairs may involve a criterion or means: by inserting a plate/I was practicing dentistry; by hitting the nail on the head/I was driving it into the wall. Or adopting a verbal means instead of verbal: by saying 'I do'/I was marrying her; by bidding 'double'/I informed him I had no clubs. Or it may have a means-to-end sense: by speaking/I convinced.

For a 'by saying' formula tests for perlocutionaries: (1) if the 'by' is instrumental versus criterial; (2) the 'saying' if fully locutionary (not just phatic) and not by double-convention (e.g., bridge bids). Subsidiary tests distinguish illocutionary from perlocutioanry, in that ILAs can be paraphrased as 'to say x is to do x,' and (can in principle) have explicit performatives, while perlocutionaries do not (I warn versus I convince).

Lecture XI contrasts performatives and constatives from the side of constatives. It had been proposed that Performatives do something, not merely state it; and that Constatives are true or false, while Performatives are ± felicitous. But stating is doing and saying, and has felicity conditions as well. Austin went through the various tests and showed how they may be qualified, particularly when we assume that the study has to do with utterances in speech situations, not in isolation. Statements require 'uptakes' that 'take effect' by committing me to other statements; and if they do not invite any response, neither do many illocutionary acts.

But granting that both statements and performatives are felicitous, the question attaches to the former more than the latter about states of affairs: mere 'endorsement' is sufficient. But VERDICTIVES have to do with truth or falsity. And the scalar *estimate—fin—pronounce* is usually qualified with *correctly*, or *wrongly*, not with *falsely*. There are also parallels among inferring and arguing soundly or validly and stating truly; between warning and advising correctly, or praising and blaming, congratulating, etc.

It may be considered that the difference is in focus: we abstract from illocutioanry aspects in constatives and reverse our attention for performatives. The difference may be one of historical perspective. But it seemed to Austin that the two must be distinguished and defined, in ways they can be intended and judged, first to be in order, and then to be 'right' or 'wrong' in their own spheres. Phatic and rhetic acts are, of course, abstractions, for every genuine act of speech is a speech act, and different kinds of nonsense are appropriate to each. This should remind us that statements, too, are ideals.

Lecture XII can now distinguish a general from a special theory, justified by the assumption that the only *actual* phenomenon is an act of speech, about which we can inquire with profit as to dimensions of felicity, illocutionary force, truth, and locutionary meaning (sense and reference). It would seem that the original project of making a list of performative verbs should yield to the larger one of listing *illocutionary forces* of utterances. But the distinction of *primary* and *explicit* performatives ought to survive, while the notion of *pure* performatives probably cannot. We need more families and fewer dichotomies.

Austin proposed the following types by illocutionary force:

1. Verdictives
2. Exercitives
3. Commissives
4. Behabatives
5. Expositives

1. Verdictives give finding of value or fact; 2. Exercitives exercise authority; 3. Commissives promise or commit; 4. Behabatives are social and attitudinal; 5. Expositives explain how utterances fit, (and he finds most difficulty with the last two):

> To sum up, we may say that the verdictive is an exercise of judgement, the exercitive is an assertion of influence or exercising of power, the commissive is an assuming of an obligation or declaring of an intention, the behabative is the adopting of an attitude and the expositive the clarifying of reason, arguments and communications (Austin 1962:161).

To this Austin appended further explanations of the types and long lists of verbs proposed for membership in each.

Searle on Speech Acts

Searle took Austin's work as his point of departure. Speech acts for him include making statements, threats, promises, questions and the like, and are the unit of communication. From them we can abstract elements for separate treatment, such as propositional content, reference, and prediction, so that the basic dichotomy is between PROPOSITIONAL CONTENT and ILLOCUTIONARY FORCE.

So his problem was the classification of forces, and he proposed norms (which he found, like Austin, tend to fade into each other). These are:

(1) The POINT or PURPOSE of an utterance.

(2) The DIRECTION OF FIT of the utterance (i.e. words-to-world or world-to-words?). This would be his ideal, but he couldn't make it work.

(3) EXPRESSED PSYCHOLOGICAL STATE in the performance of an ILA: belief, regret, wish, etc. (one of which is involved, even when sincerity is lacking.)A technique would be to see what kinds of verb expressions like 'belief, intention, desire, pleasure' collect.

(4) DEGREE OF FORCE or COMMITMENT. Strength distinguishes *suggest* and *insist*, although he found the content to be the same.

(5) STATUS of the SPEAKER and HEARER.

(6) Relation of the utterance to INTERESTS OF SPEAKER AND HEARER, as seen in boasting, lamenting, condoling, congratulating. This makes the content good or bad.

(7) Difference in DISCLOSURE RELATIONS which relate to other utterances like 'I reply, deduce, conclude.'

(8) Differences in PROPOSITIONAL CONTENT determined by ILLOCUTIONARY force, as in contrasts of reports and predictions.

(9)NON-LINGUISTICALLY performable versus LINGUISTI-CALLY performable only.

(10) INSTITUTIONAL REQUIREMENTS for expressions like 'You're fired.'

While these are interesting, Searle found that they are not all equally useful:

(1) states the essential condition;
(2) follows from (1) as an immediate, not an essential consequence;
(3 is included in sincerity conditions, while
(5) and (6) are preparatory conditions;
(4) is probably carried by essential conditions, while
(7) and (8) are probably carried by them too;
(9), (10) and (11) do not seem to be carried that way.

Searle found Austin's list unsatisfactory and confused on several grounds. One objection is that he included in his list verbs that are not illocutionary at all: e.g., 'Sympathize, I am determined to, regard as, mean to, intend, shall, and agree,' etc. He would accept that expressing agreement is illocutionary, but not the verb 'agree.'

Many of the definitions Austin gave of the categories do not always fit all members, or if they do, it is because they are taken very vaguely, as one must in order to accept the class of BEHABATIVES. Other dubious choices are 'describe' and 'identify,' which appear both as VERDICTIVES and EXPOSITIVES. He doubted that 'defy' and 'challenge' should be grouped with 'apologize' and 'congratulate.'

Searle's Taxonomy

The labels are not important. But Searle thought that his norms DISTINGUISH speech acts, and he supplied formal notation (not included here) for them:

(1) REPRESENTATIVE: these commit the speaker to something being the case, i.e. to the truth of the proposition, so the direction of fit will be 'words-to-world' and expressed psychological state is *Belief* about propositional content. Searle thought that this includes most of Austin's EXPOSITIVES and many VERDICTIVES. Added qualifiers would be degrees of commitment.

(2) IMPERATIVE: a bit strong, perhaps, Searle admitted, butdefinable as 'attempts of the speaker to get the hearer to do something, either modest or fierce, so the fit will be *'world to words'* and the psychological state, *Desire* about the propositional content. This includes 'order, request, command, beg, entreat, ask, question, pray,' etc.

(3) COMMISSIVE: Austin's class is correct, and Searle had no suggestions: defined as 'undertakings by the speaker, i.e. the speaker commits himself to a future course of action.' Fit is from *'world to words,'* and the sincerity condition will be INTENTION involving the propositional content. He would have liked to collapse (2) and

(3) on the basis of sameness of fit, but could not do it, since he could not show a promise is a kind of command to oneself.

(4) EXPRESSIVE: here, the purpose of an act is to express a psychological state, as in thanks, apologies, etc. There is *no direction of fit* for propositional content, since the truth of the proposition is presented as presupposed, and we are neither attempting to get the world to fit the proposition nor the proposition to fit the world. Psychological state varies with the kind of act: thanks in gratitude, pleasure in congratulations, and sorrow in condolence.

(5) DECLARATIVE: defined as 'alternation of status or a condition by declaration': that is, when I say 'You're fired,' the change is a result of my declaring it. These do not seem to demand a sincerity condition or an expressed psychological state, so *all we have is the propositional content.* The direction of fit is interesting: while Declaratives attempt to bring about a change in the world, like commands and promises, they automatically bring about what they change, as it were, by the utterance. If the speech act is successful, you are indeed fired. By contrast, a command may be successfully performed, without guaranteeing a change in the world, and something like that holds for promises.

Searle intuited that, if he is onto a correct classification, there should be syntactic consequences, but these have yet to be discovered. Also, he did not think that his work constituted a rejection of Austin's, who he thought was on the right track; but in defining set I and V the way he did, he thought that he was utilizing two subsidiary features to define the REPRESENTATIVE class: Set I will be the evidential and authoritative standing of the speaker, and V will depend on whether there is a discourse relational marker. Austin's is, therefore, a variation on the more fundamental taxonomy he proposes. In IV, Searle would have preferred to put 'defy' and ' challenge' under his own class of IMPERA-TIVE and not in the class of 'apologize' and the like. Again, he thought that forms Austin classified under EXERCITIVES and VERDICTIVES fit under his DECLARATIVE.

But there are overlaps: e.g., 'appoint' does not seem to fit with 'order, request, urge' or 'command' (and in all these cases, Searle expected syntactic consequences). Some of the DECLARATIVE overlap with REPRESENTATIVE. The reason is that we do not, in some circumstances, just want to establish the facts, but to have someone in authority spell them out, so that the discussion and arguments come to an end. That's why we have referees and umpires and judges: when the judge says 'You're guilty,' he is indeed making a REPRESENTATIVE claim; but it is also at the same time a DECLARATIVE, since the effects in law follow. The umpire might be mistaken, but his decision is final.

This has caused confusion in the Philosophy of Law: one school of legal realism holds that if you want to know what the Law IS, see what judges have decided. But from the judges' point of view, they have to figure out a case on the basis of what the Law IS.

Study of surface structures can be EMPIRICAL in an immediate, sensory interpretation; study of deep structures (semantic or syntactic) cannot. It is 'mediately' empirical by intersubjective agreement among native speakers that the 'deep' EXPLAINS the 'surface.' Intralinguistic PRESUPPOSITIONS (e.g., the implication between *on* versus *under*; hyponymous *flower* versus *rose*; Process 'live' and State 'dead,' differ from extralinguistic ones (e.g., speaker's intentions, possible (mis)interpreted contexts). Hence, the need for the study of SPEECH ACTS and PERFORMATIVES.

Speech Acts in the Songs

An examination of the texts of the American University Alma Mater and Fight Song makes it possible to delineate the following types of speech acts inherent in them:

Speech Act Type	Alma Mater	Fight Song
1. Representative	(a) Friendship will always bind us and remind us of Red, White and Blue!	
2. Imperative	(a) …Recalling days that flew so fast (b) Come, come days, that we treasure, we live in you! (c) Come, days, fullest in measure of our AU!	(a) So lets all join in and give a yell for AU and victory!
3. Commissive		(a) When there's a fight we'll see it through! (b) You can be sure we'll be triumphant, when we wear red, white and blue.

(c) We'll conquer
ev'ry enemy!

4. Expressive   (a) We yearn now   (a) All hail the mighty
for all the   AU Eagles!
pleasures of
college we knew!

Coincidentally, each song has five speech acts. The Alma Mater has one representative, three imperative and one expressive speech acts. The Fight Song has one imperative, three commissive and one expressive speech acts. None of the songs has a declarative speech act.

The representative speech act seeks to commit one to friendship beyond college days. It is triggered by the verbs "bind" and "remind." The imperative speech acts attempt to get one to recall and treasure the days at and to cheer for American University. These are triggered by the verbs "recalling," "come," "treasure," "live," "join," and "yell." The commissive speech acts seek to get one to commit herself/himself to fight for, wear the colors of, conquer the enemy of and hail American University athletic teams. These are triggered by the verbs "fight," "wear," "conquer," and "hail." The expressive speech act conveys a psychological state of the pleasures one gets while at American University. This is triggered by the verb "yearn."

Reflections

In light of the ideas discussed in the preceding sections of this chapter, how, or whether, the study of Performatives fit into the general field of Linguistics may not be clear. But it would be a mistake to dismiss them because they cannot fit at all, or only because combined with difficulty in a particular model or theory in Linguistics. The object of Linguistics is language, and any contribution should be assimilable.

The title 'To Kill a Mockingbird' abbreviates an adage quoted in the book of that name, that 'It's a sin to kill a mockingbird' (because mockingbirds harm no one and give pleasure to anyone willing to listen). That book criticized the sport children found in harassing a gentle, mentally retarded, neighbor. *Criticize* is a factive verb accepted without criticism when the presuppositions of speakers and hearers agree. Durkheim called such agreement a Social Fact.

De Saussure saw 'conventional simplification of the data' as a prerequisite for scientific study. By abstracting from the expression of an adage like the one just quoted, separate studies about (1) the ways things are, (2) ways they are understood, and (3) ways language must express them, the Modistae proposed a kind of Instrumental View of language: none of the three modes mentioned is actually autonomous, but Linguistics focuses mainly on Mode (3).

The study of Speech Acts works with a combination of (2) and (3). But when Truth (rather than just Validity) becomes a concern in a logic of Presuppositions, some convention about how to use data from (1) is needed. It does not seem promising to expect Linguistics to provide the definite answer to such questions. In practice, linguists take common sense and the findings of contemporary science for granted.

These modes were distinguished by abstracting from concrete utterances, just like grammatical categories can be studied independently of actual words, but each perspective helps us appreciate the role of the other. It is not easy to avoid fusing them, or to be so interested in one that it seems to be the whole. In the *The New Grammarians' Funeral: A Critique of Noam Chomsky's Linguistics* (1978), for instance, Ian Robinson said that the study of Speech Acts is a standing rebuke to Chomsky's work, which he said is focused on a putative Competence rather than attested Use. Robinson agreed with Wittgenstein that ordinary language is perfectly in order, and in no need of abstract propositional or Competence studies: language Use is what language 'means.'

An instrumental view does not disagree with that: Language doesn't 'mean' anything, people do. We use it as a tool. But some tools are perfectly designed for a job, others work more or less, and others just won't do. Linguists study language and its parts to find out what works well and what doesn't work at all—and why. Grammatical theories and models are tools to study tools, with the same design problems.

Speakers are judged to use surface structures of language as a tool, aptly, perversely, or imaginatively, by other speakers. Linguistics can give one account of why what works well for one speaker may fail another, since language is not a personal tool like a pocket knife for many uses, but a social tool like jumbo jet, with conventionally restricted employment. When Alice suggested that Humpty Dumpty's problem was whether a word could mean just what he wanted it to mean, he retorted that the real problem was, 'Who's in charge?' A Dialectician as social critic takes for granted that Society determines what language, its parts, and acceptable manipulation *do* or *can* mean.

What is the 'basic' Use of Language? Various authors and disciplines have different answers: Logicians see fixing the conditions for valid inference as most important; some Rhetoricians found persuasion more important than truth; Poets know that beauty is truth, while Anthropologists or Sociologists can find language is our prime tool for survival at any level of civilization, beside which other questions are academic. Is man social because he is rational, or rational because he is social? 'Reading maketh the full man.'

A cognitive approach is most compatible with the logician's assumption that rational discourse is basic, as well as with the anthropologist's decision to record what an objective observer must notice, without invoking unobservable value-systems. We are rated on a continuum, with 'logical' or 'useful' at one end, through harmless to insane at the other, depending largely on the coherence of what we say. Even without certainty about 'the way things are,' some match exists between the ways language is taken to mean and the ways we think is taken for granted.

Not every utterance is taken as true or false, but as appropriate on that continuum, and on yet another scale based on social, poetic, rhetorical, and 'civilized' norms: as with (1), (2), (3), those modes may all be actually one, but worth distinguishing.

'Break a leg!'

Chapter 8

Conclusions

In this chapter, I present a résumé of ideas which emerged during my preoccupation with this work. As always, in the application of academic ideas to vital documents such as academically-symbolic texts, there is the very real possibility of the premature acceptance of untested concepts and theories. The analyst must, therefore, shoulder the responsibility of pointing out the limitations of current approaches (as is done in the preceding chapters) and to demonstrate the empirical basis for the working categories employed. It is for this reason that this book surveyed many approaches in linguistic pragmatics in a depth that makes such limitations clearer.

The analyses in the preceding chapters show that pragmatic analyses can be glossed as 'covert factors making the overt coherent.' Real-world factors determined the intralinguistic, grammatical choices of the composers of the songs studied. Social-world factors covertly determined their overt, intralinguistic grammars differently.

Since semantic representation should be able to identify tautologies, contradictions, anomalies and paraphrases, it must be able to compare *given* (overt, occurrent) bits with the rest of language, infinite resources which are covert, non-occurrent. This pairing task can appear simple at a categorical competence level, daunting at the boundaries of lexical, contextualized performance level.

Presupposition, for instance, can designate a state, process or action. These three possibilities correspond to some ambiguities in linguists' use of that expression. Presupposition may be coherently said to *inhere* in language viewed as a state, to *emerge* in language viewed as a process, or to be something languages cause when considered as actions. Questions about presupposition become relevant or unanswerable, depending on these points of view.

We can ask if a state is absolute or relative, inherent or resultant from a process or an action; or process, we can ask under what conditions they occur. We ask who is responsible for actions and effects of instruments. Questions that have been raised, therefore, have included (a) Who or what presupposes? (b) What is covert and overt? and (c) What is to be said about overt expressions for which only overt incoherence can be found? Notice that "coherence" sidesteps vexing questions about "truth."

Distinguishing sense and reference involves different norms for determining synonymy and its consequences in semantic interpretation of truth-conditions. If existence (a basic concern in presuppositions) must be decided on empirical testability, differences about "truth" and "meaning" are predictable. While a normative solution to these questions is not obvious, some of the sources of confusion are. By examining the terms involved, and some assumptions of linguists considered in this book, the danger of confusing a gloss with a translation can be pointed out, if not avoided. In this perplexing area, a short sketch can prepare only for caution, not sure interpretation.

In non-technical usage, the terms imply, infer, and entail are often used indiscriminately. Sometimes, it is clear that (a) the point of view shifts from viewing language as a state, process or action, and (b) from viewing language as an Agent to that of an Instrument employed by an Agent. Once this stance has been identified, the status of presuppositions is still to be determined as coherent or incoherent within each metaphor. Distinctions commonly recognized involve norms such as

(a) overt versus covert, (b) simultaneous versus successive, with the priorities in either based on time, logic, psychologically explicit advertence and the like.

In general usage, a covert *Implication* can be distinguished from an overt *assertion* and an implicit *entailment* from an explicit *conclusion*. An *inference* is ambiguously contained in texts or made by people. Both *implicatures* and *inferences* can be inexplicit in textual or human terms, while a *deduction* is explicit in both. *Inference* can be a process or action appropriate to people who *infer*, while both texts and people can be ambiguously said to *imply*. A *deduction* can be an act or process, while deducibility is a state. All of these involve analogous (systematically ambiguous) notions of *necessity*, which involve a kind of *priority* or *simultaneity* (temporal, logical, natural). Usage is confused when the type of *necessity* or *priority* is inexplicit or undecidable.

Modern scientific statements made in the linguistic form 'If…then' can be referred to as implicatures. This *form* is a Constant; what might fill it, variables. The constant formal relations are independent of the material (substantive) nature of variables filling them, so formal validity and truth are inextricably related, in that, given true premises and a valid form, a conclusion must be true.

Stated this way, a *system* is presented as a network of dependence (e.g., grammatical and phonological systems) and a *system of systems* (a meta-system per se) allows both for independent and interdependent relations between them. Presupposition currently looks particularly to the syntax of what is overtly asserted and covertly taken for granted in a true or false context. Linguistic pragmatic usage involves contexts where truth or falsity are not involved, but appropriateness is in question.

This is a point at which ambiguity necessarily arises. But ambiguity can be shown to be systematic, and a term like "presuppose" analogical, if its sense (and possible reference) can be established as clear in a defining environment and the differences calculated from the defining differences of other environments. The clearest logical instance is *existential presupposition*; less clear are grammatical, social, psychological, and other factors which are demanded, tolerated or excluded in semantic interpretation.

Assuming normal, unmarked, non-contrastive sentences which do not *assert* existence, a subject is taken as old information (so can be presupposed), a predicate as new (so normally asserted). Without a distinction of *sense* and *reference*, anomalies arise when the sole norm of truth and falsity is referential. Sentences consisting of words that have independent 'sense' allow at least a grammatical presupposition of "existence" identical in affirmation and negation, but if that is excluded referentially in the assertion, its negation must be logically 'true': if an assertion is 'false,' its negation must be 'true.'

Necessities of language can be distinguished from those of real-world conditions, and both from psychological constructs. Even scientific theories properly 'reside' in thought where their substantial condition is conceptual; both this abstracted status and the states of affairs to which they can be reduced are different from the conventions of language in which they are expressed. Logicians now employ the notion of "possible worlds," within which real-world incoherence (and truth or falsity defined in those terms) can be neutralized, so stressing the formality of their enterprise. It reminds one of the time when Nuclear Bombs only 'existed' in physicists' heads.

So, the first matter of the American University Alma Mater and Fight Song we ought to consider is the dual nature of these songs: (a) as an aesthetic human experience, which not only give pleasure but also teach life in varying degrees of intensity (an individual re-creates what has been created by the composers); and (2) as the object of study, or of our intellectual curiosity. One might well ask the professor of American University whether in his/her teaching, and even in his/her research, s/he recognizes the inseparable nature of these aspects of the American University Alma Mater and Fight Song.

The songs can no longer be considered merely an adventitious or decorative object in life or in culture; they must be seen rather as some of the deepest expressions of the ethos of a people. Professors at American University cannot ignore this reality: the American University songs are *life*, readily available to the hearer/reader and full of humanizing tension. If the songs are a transcendental aesthetic experience which not only is *present* in the 'then' and 'there' of the texts and the feelings of the composers but can also *be moving toward* the 'here' and 'now' of the hearer/reader, then, the American University student ought to be considered first of all as a *hearer/reader*. And in order to help him/her be a real hearer/reader—the best possible hearer/reader, we have to make him/her see that being such a hearer/reader comes near to being a writer: a writer or an author in the widest meaning of the word, but in a passive sense one who re-creates in his/her hearing/reading what was felt and intuited by the original, active authors.

We might propose as a starting point that all studies of school songs, even on the most elementary levels, aim at the following objectives. First, we must stress the uniqueness of the school song-aesthetic experience, an act of school song per se; and recognize that to fail to enter into the imaginative song of 'writer-hearer/reader' may be whatever else one wishes, but most certainly is not to come to grips with the essence of the songs. To abstain from this aesthetic experience of being a 'participant' is, in the final analysis, not to study the songs.

Second, we should give the hearer/reader such scholarly assistance (historical, philosophical, sociological, political, and linguistic contexts, etc.) as may be necessary to illustrate and help him/her understand and place the text in the 'then' and 'there' in which it was conceived. But all effort along these lines ought to be subordinate to the first one, the aesthetic purpose.

Finally, we should orient the hearer/reader of the songs in the search for ethical implications which all works pose. The moral responsibility (or irresponsibility) of an author is inseparable from his/her aesthetic vision. In this way the hearer/reader would examine the value of the text in a dual perspective—ethical and aesthetic—and new dimensions would be added to the traditional historical-musicological analysis.

To study school songs in this way as a deeply-rooted manifestation of life would lead to a better understanding of the customs, the social institutions, and the individual historical events of academic institutions. The songs would also provide an approach to the visual arts, whose deeper meanings often escape the eye of the uninitiated observer because of his/her tendency to isolate cultural phenomena from their context in order to judge them in the context of his/her own culture where these phenomena may have little or no meaning or a totally mistaken one.

We ought never to falsify the cultural reality (life, art, literature) which is the goal of the student's study. We would, thus, have to oppose all sorts of simplified, or supposedly simplified, texts and stress instead the methods which will achieve the best possible access to real life, language and music.

The observations I have made in this chapter are not directed at the discovery of any method or pedagogical panacea. I present them in complete modesty in the belief that what matters most is not the method but the professor. May my observations serve then, at best, as a starting point for that self-examination. Since teaching about the American University phenomenon is one to which many of us are deeply committed, I venture to address my colleagues in the profession with the hope that they will not only give serious consideration to my suggestions and perplexities, but also strive to suggest better solutions than those I have here proposed.

Bibliography

Alston, W. P. 1964. *The Philosophy of Language.* Englewood Cliffs, New Jersey: Prentice-Hall.

American University Alumni Directory 1999. 1999. White Plains, New York: Bernard C. Harris Publishing Company.

Arnold, G. X. and D. Ros. (no date, in progress). *American University History.*

Austin, J. L. 1962. *How to do Things with Words.* New York, NY: Oxford University Press.

Babbie, E. 1992. *The Practice of Social Research* 6th ed. Belmont, California: Wadsworth Publishing Company.

Bangura, A. K. 2000. Divisive barbarity or national civilization: Linguistic presuppositions of the Sierra Leone National Anthem as a teaching tool for peaceful behavior. *International Journal of Sierra Leone Studies & Reviews* 1, 1:71-82.

Bangura, A. K. 1997. *The Presuppositions and Implicatures of the Founding Fathers.* Larchmont, New York: Cummings & Hathaway Publishers.

Bangura, A. K. 1996. *Political Presuppositions and Implicatures of the Most Popular African-American Hymns.* Commack, New York: Nova Science Publishers.

Bangura, A. K. and M. O. Thomas. 1998. *Bowie State University Alma Mater: Historical Context and Linguistic Presuppositions.* Washington, DC: The African Institution Publications.

Bartlett, F. C. 1932. *Remembering.* Cambridge, England: Cambridge University Press.

Bateson, G. 1972. *Steps to an Ecology of Mind.* New York, New York: Ballantine Books.

Brown, G. 1977. *Listening to Spoken English.* London, England: Longman.

Brown, P. and S. C. Levinson. 1978/1987. *Politeness: Some Universals in language Usage.* Cambridge, England: Cambridge University Press.

Brown, G. and G. Yule. 1983. *Discourse Analysis.* Cambridge, England: Cambridge University Press.

Carnap, R. 1942. *Introduction to Semantics.* Cambridge, Massachusetts: MIT Press.

Chafe, W. L. 1972. Discourse structure and human knowledge. In R. O. Freedle and J. B. carroll, eds. *Language Comprehension and the Acquisition of Knowledge.* Washington, DC: V. H. Winston.

Chafe, W. L. 1970. *Meaning and the Structue of Language.* Chicago, Illinois: Chicago University Press.

Charniak, E. *Towards a Model of Children's Story Comprehension.* Cambridge, Massachusetts: MIT Press, MIT Artificial Intelligence Laboratory Monographs, No. 226.

Chomsky, N. 1964. Current issues in linguistic theory. In J. Fodor and J. J. Katz, eds. *The Structure of Language.* Englewood Cliffs, New Jersey: Prentice-Hall.

Chomsky, N. 1959. On certain formal properties of grammar. *Information and Control* 2:137-167.

Cobb, R. and C. Elder. 1976. Symbolic identification and political behavior. *American Politics Quarterly* 4.

Copi, I. and C. Cohen. 1994. *Introduction to Logic*. New York, New York: Macmillan Publishing Company.

Dahl, O. 1969. *Topic and Comment: A Study of Russian and Transformational Grammar*. Goteborge, Sweden: Slavica Gothoburgensia 4.

De Beaugrande, R. 1980. *Text Discourse and Process*. London, England: Longman.

Descrates, R. 1968 ed. *Philosophical Works* (in two volumes). E. S. Haldane and G. R. T. Ross (translators). Cambridge, England: The University Press.

Edelman, M. 1964. *The Symbolic Uses of Politics*. Urbana, Illinois: The University of Illinois Press.

Elder, C. and R. Cobb. 1983. *The Political Uses of Symbols*. New York, New York: Longman.

Filmore, C. J. 1975. An alternative to checklist theories of meaning (proceedings of the first annual meeting of the Berkeley Linguistic Society, University of california).

Filmore, C. J. 1968. The case for case. In E. bach and R. Harms, eds. *Universals in Linguistic Theory*. New York, New York: Holt, Rinehart and Winston.

Fogelin, R. 1967. *Evidence and Meaning*. New York, New York: Humanities Press.

Frege, G. 1892/1952. On sense and reference. In P. T. Geach and M. Black, eds. *Translations from the Philosophic Writings of Gottlob Frege*. Oxford, England: Blackwell.

Garfinkel, H. 1967. *Studies in Ethnomethodology*. Cambridge, England: Polity Press.

Gazdar, G. 1979. *Pragmatics: Implicature, Presupposition and Logical Form*. New York, New York: Academic Press.

Givon, T. 1979. *On Understanding Grammar*. New York, New York: Academic Press.

Goffman, E. 1974. *Frame Analysis*. New York, New York: Harper and Row.

Grice, H. P. 1981. Presupposition and conversational implicature. In P. Cole, ed. *Radical Pragmatics*. New York, New York: Academic Press.

Grice, H. P. 1978. Further notes on logic and conversation. In P. Cole, ed. *Syntax and Semantics 9: Pragmatics*. New York, New York: Academic Press.

Grice, H. P. 1975. Logic and conversation. In P. Cole and J. L. Morgan eds. *Syntax and Semantics: vol. 3: Speech Acts*. New York, New York: Academic Press.

Grice, H. P. 1968. Utterer's meaning, sentence-meaning, and word-meaning. *Foundations of Language* 4:1-18.

Grice, H. P. 1957. Meaning. *Philosophical Review* lxvi:377-388.

Gunn, G. 1992. Interdisciplinary studies. In J. Gibaldi, ed. *Introduction to Scholarship in Modern Languages and Literatures*. New York, New York: The Modern Languages Association of America.

Harman, G. H. 1986/1989. *Change in View*. Cambridge, Massachusetts: MIT Press.

Harman, G. H. 1968. Three levels of meaning. *The Journal of Philosophy* lxv:590-602.

Heritage, J. 1984. *Garfinkel and Ethnomethodology*. Cambridge, England: Polity Press.

Hofmann, Th. R. *Realms of Meaning*. London, England: Longman.

Hughes, J. and L. P. Cain. 1994. *American Economic History*. New York, NY: HarperCollins Publishers.

Hume, R. D. 1992. Texts within contexts: Notes toward a historical method. *Philological Quarterly* 71:69-100.

Jones, E. 1964. The psychology of constitutional monarchy. In E. Jones, ed. *Essays in Applied Psycho-analysis*. London, Engand: The Hogart Press.

Kaplan, A. 1964. *The Conduct of Inquiry*. San Francisco, California: Chandler Publishing Company.

Karttunen, L. 1973. Presuppositions of compound sentences. *Linguistic Inquiry* iv, 2:169-193.

Karttunen, L. 1971. Implicative verbs. *Language* 47:340-358.

Kates, C. A. 1980. *Pragmatics and Semantics: An Empiricist Theory*. Ithaca, New York: Cornell University Press.

Katz, J. J. 1966. *The Philosophy of Language*. New York, New York: Harper and Row.

Katz, J. J. and J. Fodor. 1964. *The Structure of Language*. Englewood Cliffs, New Jersey: Prentice-Hall.

Kiparsky, P. and C. Kiparsky. 1971. Fact. In D. D. Steinberg and L. A. Jakobovits, eds. *Semantics*. Cambridge, England: Cambridge University Press.

Leech, G. N. 1983. *Principles of Pragmatics*. London, England: Longman.

Kintsch, W. 1974. *The Representation of Meaning in Memory*. Hillsdale, New Jersey: Lawrence Erlbaum Publishing Company.

Levinson, S. C. 1983. *Pragmatics*. Cambridge, England: Cambridge University Press.

Lyons, J. 1977. *Semantics 1 & 2*. Cambridge, England: Cambridge University Press.

Merelman, R. 1966. Learning and legitimacy. *American Political Science Review* 60.

Meyer, B. J. F. 1975. *The Organization of Prose and Its Effects on Meaning*. Amsterdam, Holland: North Holland Press.

Morris, C. W. 1946. *Signs, language, and Behavior*. Englewood Cliffs, New Jersey: Prentice-Hall.

Morris, C. W. 1938. *Foundations of the Theory of Signs*. Chicago, Illinois: Chicago University Press.

Nachmias, D. and C. 1981. *Research Methods in the Social Sciences* 2nd ed. New York, New York: St. Martin's Press.

Patterson, A. 1992. Historical scholarship. In J. Gibaldi, ed. *Introduction to Scholarship in Modern Languages and Literatures*. New York, New York: The Modern Language Association of America.

Putnam, H. 1975. *Mind, Language and Reality* vo. 2. Cambridge, England: Cambridge University Press.

Reynolds, J. R. and J. E. King. 1976. *Highlights in the History of The American University, 1889-1976*. Washington, DC: Hennage Creative Printers.

Roark, J. L. et al. 2000. *The American Promise: A History of the United States*. Boston, MA: Bedford/St. Martin's Press.

Robinson, I. 1978. *The New Grammarians' Funeral: A Critique of Noam Chomsky's Linguistics*. New York, NY: Cambridge University Press.

Russell, B. 1957. Mr. Strawson on referring. *Mind* 66.

Russell, B. 1905. On denoting. *Mind* 14.

Schank, R. C. and R. Abelson. 1977. *Scripts, Plans, Goals and Understanding*. Hillsdale, New Jersey: Lawrence Erlbaum Publishing Company.

Schiffrin, D. 1987. Discovering the context of an utterance. *Linguistics* 25:11-32.

Searle, J. R. 1985. Indirect speech acts. *Language and Society* 14:58-82.

Searle, J. R. 1976. A classification of illocutionary acts. *Language and Society* 5:1-24.

Searle, J. R. 1968. *Speech Acts*. New York, NY: Cambridge University Press.

Sellars, W. 1954. Presupposing. *Philosophical Review* 63:197-215.

Stalnaker, R. C. 1978. Assertion. In P. Cole, ed. *Syntax and Semantics 9: Pragmatics*. New York, New York: Academic Press.

Stalnaker, R. C. 1974. Pragmatic presuppositions. In M. K. Munitz and P. K. Unger, eds. *Semantics and Philosophy*. New York, New York: New York University Press.

Steinberg, D. D. and L. A. Jakobovits. 1971. *Semantics*. Cambridge, England: Cambridge University Press.

Strawson, P. F. 1952. *Introduction to Logical Theory*. London, England: Metheun.

Strawson, P. F. 1950. On referring. *Mind* 59.

Taylor, C. 1971. Interpretation and the sciences of man. *Review of Metaphysics* 25:24.

Van Dijk, T. A. 1977. *Text and Content*. London, England: Longman.

Wilson, D. and D. Sperber. 1981. On Grice's theory of conversation. In P. Werth, ed. *Conversation and Discourse*. London, England: Croom Helm.

Worff, B. L. 1956. *Language, Thought and Reality*. Cambridge, Massachusetts: MIT Press.

Ziff, P. 1967. On H. P. Grice's account of meaning. *Analysis* xxviii:1-8.

Zinn, H. 1999. *A People's History of the United States, 1492-Present* (20th anniversary edition). New Tork, NY: HarperCollins Publishers.

About the Author

Abdul Karim Bangura holds Ph.D. degrees in Political Science, Development Economics, Linguistics, and Computer Science. He is currently a researcher-in-residence at the Center for Global Peace, a professor of International Relations, the coordinator of the B.A. in International Studies–International Peace and Conflict Resolution (IPCR) focus, the coordinator of the Islamic Lecture Series, the coordinator of the National Conference on Undergraduate Research, and the advisor of the American University Undergraduate Research Association (AUURA) and the International Peace and Conflict Resolution Association (IPCRA) in the School of International Service at American University, and the director of The African Institution in Washington, DC. From 1993 to 2000, Bangura taught Political Science and International Studies, served as Special Assistant to the President and Provost, and founded and directed The Center for Success at Bowie State University. He also has taught at Georgetown University, Howard University and Sojourner-Douglass College. He is the author of 22 books and more than 230 articles in refereed journals and other sources. His recent books include *DC Vote: Fight Against Taxation Without Representation (2001)*, *Computer Programming to Insure Project Accountability in Africa* (2001), *United States-African Relations: The Reagan-Bush Era* (2001), *United States Congress and Bilingual Education* (2001), *Historical Political Economy of Washington, DC* (2000), and *Chaos Theory and African Fractals* (2000). His recent articles and book chapters include "Business Communication in Sierra Leone: A Diglossic Model" (*The Journal of African Communication* 2001), "Measurable Effects of Societal Multilingualism in Africa"

(*International Journal of the Sociology of Language* 2000), "Divisive Barbarity or National Civilization: Linguistic Presuppositions of the Sierra Leone National Anthem as a Tool to Teach Peaceful Behavior" (*International Journal of Sierra Leone Studies and Reviews* 2000), "Articles on Africa in the *Journal of Third World Studies*: A Content Analysis and an Annotated Bibliography" (*Journal of Third World Studies* 2000), "Ethnicity's Threat to Peace" (in Elias and Turpin 1999), and "Metaphors of Global Ethics: An African Spiritual and Religious Perspective" (in Bushrui et al. 1999). He also is Editor-In-Chief of both the *Journal of Research Methodology and African Studies* (JRMAS) and the *African Journal of Languages and Linguistics* (AJLL). Bangura is the President of the Association of Third World Studies and a member of many other scholarly organizations. He has received numerous teaching and other scholarly and community service awards, and he is fluent in about a dozen African and six European languages.